A Hitch In Time

A HiTCH In TiMe

Andy Smart

ABOUT THE AUTHOR

Andy Smart is an English comedian, actor,
improvisation artist and writer.

A performer with The Comedy Store Players in London
for many years, he has been a permanent member of
the group since 1995. In the 1980s, he was one half of
'The Vicious Boys' with Angelo Abela. Together they
won the 1984 *Time Out* Street Entertainer Award
and later appeared on the cult TV show *The Tube*.

Andy has performed at 40 consecutive Edinburgh
festivals and is a regular guest on TalkSport Radio.
He lives in London and can be seen on stage at
The Comedy Store in Soho every Wednesday and
Sunday night, doing improvisation.

Published by AA Media Limited in 2019.

Text © Andy Smart 2019.
The right of Andy Smart to be identified as author
of this work has been asserted by him in accordance with
the Copyright, Designs and Patents Act 1988.

A CIP catalogue record for this book is available from
the British Library.

ISBN: 978-0-7495-8189-3

Publisher: Phil Carroll
Editor: Donna Wood
Art Director: James Tims
Designer: Tracey Freestone

Printed and bound by CPI Group (UK) Ltd, Croydon CR0 4YY

A05700

theAA.com

To Keith and Shirley Smart.
The best parents a boy could have.

Contents

Prologue

*I was surprised, as always, by how easy
the act of leaving was, and how good it felt.
The world was suddenly rich with possibility.*

JACK KEROUAC

Jack Kerouac has a lot to answer for. I read *On The Road* when I was 18 and I fell in love with hitch-hiking. Between 1977 and 1982 I hitched over 72,000 miles, in Britain, France, Germany, Holland and Spain. I became very good at it. I kept a log of everyone who picked me up over those five years, which allowed me to work out good junctions or service stations to get dropped off at.

It taught me when to turn down lifts going not quite where I was heading, and that junction 7 on the M6 is the worst in the country for catching a lift (there used to be so much graffiti on the back of the sign there – plaintive prayers and sad laments from hikers who had been there for hours). I also logged the type of lift: lorry/van – 621; car – 749; motorbike

– 2. For instance, my first and only lift in a Rolls-Royce was from the Avonmouth junction on the M5 to the Worcester turn-off. There were 1,384 lifts, of which 14 were from women. I met some wonderful people – those who put me up for the night, those who bought me meals and those who took me across the Channel for free in their lorry cabs. There were some very strange ones, and a couple of downright scary ones. But I wouldn't have missed a single one of them.

This is the story of the biggest trip I took. I'd been at college in Liverpool for four years, then spent a year on the dole and a year working in a TiE (Theatre in Education) group. But I wasn't happy. I was in love – unrequited – with someone who was with someone else, I'd watched Liverpool burn during the riots, and I wanted to be a comic. I needed a change.

Both my grandfathers were big travellers. My dad's dad, Fred Smart, was born in 1881 and joined the army at the age of 16 – he was missing his brother, who had gone to fight in South Africa. Unfortunately, he arrived to find that his brother had been moved on to India, but he spent the last two years of the Boer War fighting there.

My mum's dad, Harry Cobb, had been in the Merchant Navy, travelling the seven seas, and also fought in both world wars in the Royal Navy. In fact, his ship was sunk by a U-boat on the Baltic Fleet run to Leningrad. My dad was a civil engineer and drove all over the UK and Ireland checking new buildings. He took my mum to Madrid on the back of his BSA motorbike just after they were married, visiting a lot of the places mentioned in this book. So travel was in my blood. And I still say that travel is the best education – it definitely improved my French! I learned more in the month I was away on this trip than in the whole six years at school.

I knew that I wanted to be a comedian, but I didn't know how to go about it. Today, I could have signed up for a number of courses in stand-up or improvisation, but back then there were just the working men's clubs. Alternative comedy was raising its head and taking its first stumbling steps in 1982. This was a sort of punk comedy, where anyone could get up and perform in rooms over pubs – a mixture of agitprop theatre and Speakers' Corner, with a nod to the Pythons and the Goons. There were only three rules: you couldn't be racist, homophobic or sexist. It hadn't really reached Liverpool, though, unless you include Ken Campbell's *The Warp* at the Everyman Theatre, in which I helped turn the audience around on movable seating areas.

My theatrical debut had taken place 21 years earlier in 1961, when, at the age of two, I played Noddy in the Portsmouth Methodist Church's Christmas show.

I sang a four-line song about a golliwog. Please don't judge me – it was a different time. But I do remember the reaction. There was a lot of laughter as I repeated my verse three times. I loved it and was hooked.

I have included many more stories of my stage appearances throughout the book – some highs, some lows – and it could also be titled 'How I Got Started In Show Business'. It was all by luck, really. A bit like hitch-hiking. You just say 'Yes' and see where you end up. And I suppose I still think like that today.

Having spent the first three years of my life in Portsmouth, where I'd been born, we moved to Farnborough. I have few memories of those first three years, other than being Noddy, falling in the fish pond at my third birthday party, and the cheers from the crowd at Moneyfields football ground across the road from our house. I loved a hat in those days. Oh, and whelks.

On Friday nights my dad had a poker night with his mates while their wives would meet up at someone else's house. I would be allowed to sit at the table in my high chair. To keep me quiet when I was teething, my dad would give me a large whelk straight from the fridge and I would chew and suck it for hours while they drank, smoked and played cards.

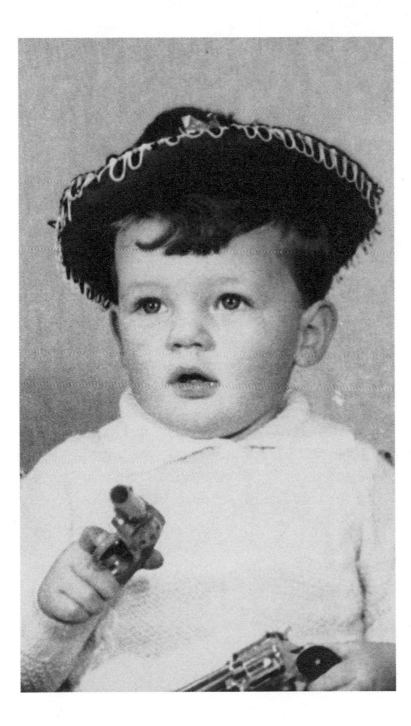

My brother Neil arrived in 1961. Although he was two years younger, from the age of six he was the same height as me. This, and the fact that my mum always dressed us the same, meant that we were always mistaken for twins. To be honest, he was cleverer than me and better at football too, but I got the looks. He has always been there for me even though our paths took us in opposite directions. He became a vet after seven years of study at Bristol, and then gave it all up later to become a vicar.

The last addition to our little family was Rosalind, who was born in August 1967. She is the kindest, most optimistic person I have ever met, and a constant inspiration.

We moved to Farnborough in the summer of 1962, and that autumn I started at Cove Manor Infant School, where I had my first brush with death. One break time, we were all out in the playground under gathering black clouds when there were a few drops of rain. The dinner ladies blew the whistle and we were told to wait for our classes to be called. As we stood waiting, a flash of lightning speared down from the firmament and hit the tarmac about 10 feet from me. Everyone within 50 feet was knocked over and there was a black scar left on the playground (there must have been a metal sewage pipe under the ground). It took the rest of the afternoon for us all to stop crying.

At the age of six I moved 200 yards across the playing field to Cove Manor Junior School. I loved my time there. I lived for the playtime football matches – to the consternation of my mother, as I went through pairs of shoes each term. It was one of these games that gave me my outlook on physical violence. In fact, it was the last time I ever punched anyone.

I was 10 years old at the time and was going through on goal when I was hacked down by a clumsy challenge by Alred Reed. I jumped to my feet, screaming for a penalty. Graham Harvey was having none of it. We argued, a circle forming around us. Graham had picked up the ball, as it was his, and was saying, 'Game over, game over!' I can remember it so clearly. The red mist descended and I gave him a right jab square in the face. I felt his nose collapse under my fist, and as I pulled my arm back I saw his look of incomprehension. Then he reached up to his nose, just as the first drops of blood started to flow. He burst into tears and ran off.

Unfortunately, Graham was the son of Mr Harvey, the deputy headmaster. We were called to his office at the end of the day and I received six across the hand with a wooden ruler. I vowed never to punch anyone again (I never said anything about headbutts, though, but that's another story).

Somehow I passed the 11-plus. I remember the last question: 'What is the line called where the sea meets the sky?' I couldn't think of the word. The teacher, Mrs Cameron, was collecting the papers and left me till last as she could see me struggling to remember.

'HORIZON!' I eventually shouted and hurriedly wrote it down.

That one mark grabbed me a place at Farnborough Grammar School. Without it, I would have gone to Cove Secondary School. So thank you, Mrs Cameron.

The grammar school was scary at first. We had a uniform that included a cap, and the older boys terrorised us by threatening to cut off the button on the top. There was a lot of bullying, but I would always answer the bully back. I figured that I was going to get a beating anyway, so I might as well get in a hurtful jibe. Also, the kids found out that I wouldn't fight back. Even in the third year I was being bullied by first years. I was also very small: I stayed at five feet tall from age

12 to 16, but then grew 11 inches in a year. Suddenly, I was taller than those who had bullied me. I had some good friends, though: Pete Carey, Ian 'Arthur' Craggs, Jimmy 'Blancmange' Bell, Steve 'Harrington Jacket' Hunter, Ian Huntingford, Steve Collins, Jonathan Bell, Chris Heald, Asko Croft, Will Tanner, Rev Williams, Tony Jenner, Nige Elms and Paul Bolt.

When I was 13 I had a paper round. I'd get the 40-odd papers from the newsagent on Giffard Drive and deliver them before cycling to school. I didn't really enjoy it – and especially not in the winter – so I was looking for an easier way of making money. I had bought my first *Mayfair* magazine while on holiday down in Christchurch, near Bournemouth. Like all boys of that age, I was curious about sex. I had no idea what went on. Sex lessons in those days consisted of pictures of the interiors of the male and female bodies, and they lasted about 20 minutes. I read that *Mayfair* cover to cover, over and over again, and I wanted to read more. But I couldn't pluck up the courage to buy another mag in case someone I knew saw me. It was a very different time then.

Now, I was always mouthy. People say they became a stand-up because they would make the bullies laugh at school, but I never quite got it right. I'd make jokes about the bully to make the others laugh, but, of course, this just resulted in harder beatings. But some of the older boys liked my attitude. After a nasty incident when two boys grabbed my legs and pulled in different directions, some fifth-formers (two years above me) came up and started talking to me. I became friends with two of them. I will not name them, but they started to supply me with 'dirty' magazines. They would buy them in the shop for 50p, I would buy them for 40p when they'd grown bored with the contents, and then I would lend them out to third years for 25p a night. There was a fine system for not bringing them back in the condition they were lent. I soon had quite a library in place and I was making enough to give up the paper round.

This went on for two terms until disaster struck that summer. It was exam time and a hot June day. The catchment area for Farnborough Grammar School was quite large: we had kids from Fleet, Ash, Camberley and Aldershot, and the kids from Aldershot were usually from army families. It was 1974 – the height of the Troubles in Northern Ireland and there were a lot of bombs being placed on the mainland in an IRA campaign. With so many boys from army families we were considered a prime target for them, but the sixth-formers who realised this could also use it to their advantage. If they weren't ready for an exam, they would sometimes ring the police with a warning, the school would have to be searched and their exam postponed.

On this day, someone rang in with a bomb threat. It was towards the end of lunch and I was playing football on the fields at the back of the school. I'd left my briefcase in our form room. We lined up on the football pitch behind the kitchens in our forms. We'd had a few of these bomb scares over the previous two weeks and no one was taking it too seriously. But this time we were kept waiting outside for quite a while. I started to wonder what was taking so long.

'They're searching bags at the moment,' said Mr Porter, our form teacher.

I went as white as a sheet. In my bag were three *Mayfairs*, five *Penthouses* and a *Fiesta*! One porn mag was enough to get you expelled from the grammar school, so what would they do to someone who had nine? It was the longest 20 minutes of my life. I was sure they were going to find them. Looking back, they probably wouldn't have been looking in our bags. But at the time, my 13-year-old self was horrified. When we were allowed back into the school, I ran to my bag and held onto it for the rest of the afternoon. Then, after school, I stood by the bike sheds and gave away all of my stock. Everything.

The following year I realised that I needed another business plan. Every other Saturday we would go to Portsmouth to see my two grandmas. There was a shop opposite my paternal grandmother's house which sold large red gobstoppers for a halfpenny each. In Farnborough, the same sweets went for 2p. So I would buy 100 gobstoppers for 50p and then sell them at break for a penny each, doubling my money.

This was OK for a while but meant carrying a lot of gobstoppers around all the time.

A few of us had started playing pontoon at break time. My gran had explained to me how it was played in casinos and had told me the house always won. So, after a few weeks, I said that I would take over the dealing but I wouldn't bet. In a week we had a three-table casino running. I provided the dealers and a lookout on the door to the corridor – usually they were boys who had lost their money and would work a couple of break times to earn some back so they could play again. I would share out the bank's winnings, keeping half for myself and dividing the rest between the dealers and the lookout. But boys began losing their lunch money and so we were given a lecture on gambling and I had to knock the casino on the head.

I did keep one form of gambling going that year. Every Tuesday, at 4.45pm on BBC1, there was a cartoon called *Wacky Races*. It portrayed the attempts of Dick Dastardly to win a car race around some part of America. There were 11 cars: Peter Perfect in the Turbo Terrific, Penelope Pitstop in the Compact Pussycat, Professor Pat Pending in the Convert-a-Car, Lazy Luke and Blubber Bear in the Arkansas Chugabug, Sergeant Blast and Private Meekly in the Army Surplus Special, Red Max in the Crimson Haybailer, the Slag Brothers (Rock and Gravel) in the Boulder Mobile, the Gruesome Twosome in the

Creepy Coupe, the Ant Hill Mob in the Bulletproof Bomb, Rufus Ruffcut and a beaver (what was that all about?) in the Buzz Wagon, and Dastardly and Muttley in the Mean Machine.

I would run a book on who would win that night's race. The Professor was always the favourite, at 6/4, as his car could turn into a boat, a helicopter or a plane. Red Max, at 2/1, won a fair few because he was in a plane. The outsiders were Dick Dastardly and Muttley, at 25/1, as they never won because they always cheated − and, as we all know, cheats never prosper (except for Brexit). One kid, who shall remain nameless, backed Dick every week − and every week I took his money.

It was no surprise, then, that I jumped at the chance when the school announced they would be offering the first chance to take an A Level in Pure Maths and Statistics. As it was the first time the course had been tried, it was implied by the teachers that there was a good chance we would all pass. I was just thrilled to be able to use my knowledge of the rules of chance for good. I was joined by my friend Pete Carey and we decided to form a club for all of us on the course. We called ourselves the StatsKings and made membership cards and badges at the school printing club. Whenever we saw another member of the StatsKings walking around school during the day, we would bellow the greeting 'Whayooooo!' We still do it to this day, 44 years later.

👍

Pete was my oldest friend. When we were four, in Cove Manor Infant School, I was picked to be the lead king in the Nativity play – I was chosen because I was the only one who walked slowly enough. Pete was my page and had to walk behind me holding the hem of my robes.

We also performed together in *The Tempest* during our lower sixth-form year. Pete was the butler, Stephano, and I played the jester, Trinculo. It was performed in the round and during the shipwreck scene (spoiler alert!) at the start of the play, Pete would be the first to fall off the ship. I would run to the rail and shout, 'Man overboard!' It isn't in the script but it always got a laugh. Then, when Ariel conjures up the hounds to chase Stephano, Trinculo and Caliban from Prospero's cave, the rest of the cast would swirl around us in dog masks creating a canine whirlpool that would take us out of the dining hall where we were performing. Just before we reached the exit I would duck down in the middle of this maelstrom and then leap high in the air, grabbing my rear and shouting, 'Aargh! Me bum!' – again, not in the script, but it got a big laugh. I loved to hear an audience laugh. I lived for it.

The next production we did was *The Caucasian Chalk Circle*. I played two roles: Jussup, who pretends

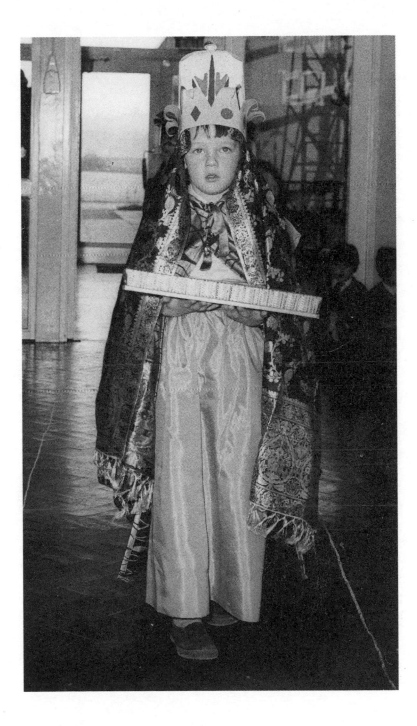

to be at death's door to avoid having to join the army, and an 80-year-old man. In the play, Grusha, who is on the run with her child, marries Jussup – the army is looking for a single mother, so she believes that they won't find her if she's married. And Jussup will probably die soon anyway and then she'll be a widow. But after the priest pronounces them man and wife, Jussup leaps up from his deathbed as he sees Grusha's beauty and wants to have his way with her. She demands that he has a bath first as he has been lying in bed for a year.

In our version, a barrel that had been cut in half was placed in the middle of the stage and I would get into it, removing my nightgown as I lowered myself. Sue Willesden, who played Grusha, was given jugs of water to pour into my bath and I would lather myself and generally make the most of having a bath in front of 400 people. It was a very funny scene and I loved it, but on the last night the other cast members left the jugs of water outside for an hour before the scene. It was February and freezing. In fact, they had to break the layer of ice on the top of each jug before they brought the water on stage. The stage direction calls for Jussup to berate Grusha for pouring water that is too hot and that scalds him. When Sue poured the first jug I squealed like a stuck pig! Somehow I got through the scene, and as I left the stage wrapped in a small towel the audience started clapping. They kept clapping after my exit and wouldn't stop until I returned and took a bow. I then made my way back to the dressing room; this was in the drama room on the other side of the quadrangle. Mr Parslew, our wonderful drama teacher (he was my form tutor as well), was waiting with my next costume.

'What was all that noise?' he asked.

'Um, they liked the bath scene,' I replied.

'Good, well, get into this. You're back on in a minute,' he said, handing me the costume. He was keeping my feet on the ground. But the laughter and the applause had affected me greatly and I knew then that I wanted to be a comedian. But I had no idea how to make that happen!

In a roundabout way Mr Parslew was responsible for my first ever hitch-hike. After A Levels I had gone on a trip to America with the Venture Scouts. Unfortunately, it clashed with the dates when Mr Parslew was taking a group of sixth-formers down to Falmouth to perform *A Midsummer Night's Dream* at a theatre there that was run by a friend of his. My girlfriend of two years, Jackie, was playing one of three Pucks. Before I left for the States we had a big heart to heart and decided that we should split up as we would both be going to university after the holidays. The relationship had run its course. I think

I secretly wanted to be free in case I met anyone in America, but nothing happened while I was there. On my return, I decided to hitch down to Falmouth and surprise her.

I walked to junction 4 of the M3, plucked up my courage and held my thumb out. I caught my first lift in about five minutes in a brown Ford Capri. The driver was in his mid-20s and was a sales rep for a firm selling windows. He took me all the way to Weymouth, where he had a meeting, and from there it took three more lifts to reach Falmouth. I walked to the theatre and bought a ticket to see the show.

The cast quickly noticed me sitting in the third row, and there was a lot of excited whispering going on. At the interval, I was approached by Mr Parslew, who was not happy to see me. He asked me why I had come and told me I would ruin the run. I didn't understand what he meant, but after the show I found out. As I waited at the stage door, the rest of the cast came out and headed for the nearest pub. Eventually Jackie emerged, holding hands with Paul Dooley. She told me that they had got together during rehearsals, since we had broken up.

I muttered something like, 'Well, I hope you'll be very happy together.' I was heartbroken. I walked back out of town and hitched back to Farnborough overnight.

It was something that occurred one Wednesday afternoon in the fourth year, though, that sums up my attitude to my time at the grammar school. The deputy head was Mr Thomas – known to everyone as Joe, when he wasn't in earshot.

Joe had been in the Africa Campaign during World War II. He took us for history, and if you ever wanted a lesson off, you just had to ask him about his fighting days against the Italians. He would go all misty-eyed and tell long stories of battles and how he and a mate had marched 2,000 POWs across the desert, just the two of them. He had joined the school straight from the army and had set up the cadet force. So, every Wednesday afternoon we played soldiers. I hated it. My main complaint was the uniforms; they had been made pre-1950, when we still had conscription, and they were invariably too big. Once a month we would have a parade on the playing fields in front of the cadet hut and an inspection by Joe himself. It was March and bitterly cold. I decided to wear my pyjamas under my uniform – a) to keep warm and b) to stop the itchiness. We gathered in our platoons on the field and had a pre-inspection by Alan Franklyn, a sadistic sixth-former who was one of the lieutenants and was hoping to join the real army when he left school.

He marched up and down the lines, telling boys to do a button up or to straighten a belt or beret. When he reached me he stopped.

'Are those pyjamas I can see under your uniform, Smart?'

'Um, yes,' I muttered.

'Yes, what?'

'Yes, sir!'

He punched me full in the stomach. I fell to the floor, winded.

'Get in that hut and take them off, then get back out here.'

I was livid. I wanted revenge. Then it came to me. I would do exactly what he had told me to do. I ran into the hut and stripped down to my Y-fronts and army boots. I looked round the door and saw that Mr Thomas was now striding, chest out, towards the parade. I ducked out of the door and took my place in the back rank where I had been standing. A lot of giggling started up around me but I shushed them to be quiet. We all stood to attention at the call.

Mr Thomas and Alan started at the far end, and as they walked the front rank I stood perfectly still. Obviously they noticed me when they started down the second rank but they carried on with the inspection. Eventually they reached my rank and began down the line towards me. Boys were openly laughing now and the front ranks were turning round to see what the commotion was all about.

Finally they reached me. Joe stood in front of me, his swagger stick under his arm and his face red with rage.

'What is the meaning of this, boy?' he asked through gritted teeth.

'Lieutenant Franklyn told me to do it. SIR!'

'He told you to do this?'

'Yes, sir! I was wearing something under my uniform and he said, "Get in that hut and take it off." He said nothing about putting anything on, sir.'

It received a huge laugh. The lines were broken as people turned round to watch and all sense of order was lost. Mr Thomas was furious, shouting orders and threatening boys with jankers (an hour walking round the playing field collecting litter). Parades were different after that, but I had got that laugh again – and I loved it. If I could do it by cocking a snook at the establishment, all the better.

In the fourth year I went on the school ski trip to Haute Savoie. I loved it. But in order to pay for it my mum and dad had to make a few sacrifices. I hadn't realised how many, until Christmas 1975 came along and one evening after school I found my mum crying in the kitchen as she made the tea. She and Dad had been having spats in the run-up to Christmas and

I hadn't put two and two together until that night. The reason she was so upset was money. They were struggling with a big mortgage but they knew how much that ski trip meant to me. I told her that I didn't want any Christmas presents. She stopped crying and hugged me.

'We'll get by,' she whispered into my hair. 'But I don't think we can afford a tree this year.'

I didn't sleep well that night. When I returned from school the next day I had a plan. After we had eaten our tea, which was the same on each day of the week (Monday was curry to use up the meat from Sunday's roast, Tuesday was beans on toast, Wednesday was gammon or pork chops, Thursday was stew in winter, salad in summer, Friday was fish, although we were not religious at all: either fish fingers, or fish and chips from the chip shop, Saturday was mince and mashed potato at lunch and sandwiches in the evening and Sunday was a full roast dinner for lunch, then whelks, winkles or cockles for tea), I grabbed my brother Neil and took him out to the garage. We took down the large wood saw from my father's work bench and headed off up West Heath Road, walking the two and a half miles to the woods round Hawley Lake.

My birthday is 16 June. This also happens to be the opening day of the coarse-fishing season in this country. Most years I got fishing gear for my birthday. I loved sitting on the banks of a river using a spinner or a float, but my favourite form of fishing was spinning for pike in Hawley Lake. I had been there the previous weekend and caught an 18-inch pike in the cold December mist.

Riding home I had noticed an area of young pine trees, and that is where we were headed. But when we arrived they didn't look like Christmas trees. Their branches were quite far apart and they had much longer needles. They were Scots pines, not Douglas fir. We eventually found one taller than both of us with a fair resemblance to a Christmas tree and I began to saw it down at the base. Dad's saw was fairly blunt, though, and it took ages. My brother and I took turns until eventually it was down.

Then came the tricky bit. We had to get it home. Neil took the front end and I held the trunk at the back in one hand with the saw in the other. We didn't look dodgy at all! We took every back route on the way home, probably adding another mile to the journey. My mum was so surprised. She started crying as we brought it into the house. I still say that was the best Christmas tree we ever had!

So, the weekend after Christmas saw me in the Alps. It was my first time in proper mountains and I bloody loved it. I learnt to ski in three days. I took more chances than the other boys, as I had no fear and I was on the Black Runs by the end of the week. I loved the fact that you use a combination of gravity, your reactions and balance to career down the piste.

We stayed in a school building at the bottom of the valley. The desks had been removed and camp beds put up in their place. In the evenings, after a communal meal, our school and the two others staying there gathered in the gymnasium to drink Coca Cola and chat about the day's skiing. There was a record player, but no one had brought any records with them, so we had to make do with three singles which were played in rotation, first the A sides, then the B sides and then back to the A sides again. One was 'Tie a Yellow Ribbon', the next was 'Crocodile Rock' and the last was a French folk song. It didn't make for a very good disco.

On New Year's Eve the locals brought a massive cake to the school. We all stayed up till midnight and sang 'Auld Lang Syne' and 'La Marseillaise'. Then we dived into the cake. No one had told us that it had been steeped in champagne. It was delicious. I had about three pieces. Everyone started drifting off to bed. But I was drunk for the first time in my life; I felt fantastic. A couple of us went outside to look at the stars, and that's when we found a pile of sledges stored in a lean-to. They were wooden with metal runners. We grabbed one each and headed to the school playing fields, which sloped away down to a road in the distance. I rushed to the top and jumped onto my sledge, then I flew down the slope, laughing maniacally.

It was a moonless night, thick with snow-carrying black clouds, and as I moved further away from the lights of the school it became harder to see what lay ahead. I knew there was a road coming up but I didn't know when. Suddenly I hit a bump and took off. I must have flown about 30 feet through the air and came down face first into a snowdrift that had built up by the fence at the roadside. I was stuck with my arms by my side in the snow. When the other boys pulled me out I was laughing like a donkey. What an adrenaline rush.

👍

When it came to O Levels in my fifth year, Mum and Dad were called to the school for a meeting with Mr Thomas. He informed them that they thought I would pass only one of my O Levels. This was based on 'Cause for Concern' (CFC), a system whereby, if a teacher thought you were underperforming, or if you disrupted the class, or if you hadn't handed homework in, then you would get a CFC. These were collected on a Friday and if you had one you had a meeting with your form tutor at first break time on Monday. If you had three CFCs, you would have to report to Mr Thomas. I can proudly say that I was the first student in the school to receive CFCs in all eight subjects.

Looking back, I always did things differently – I never wrote things down, I just listened in lessons. I was the class joker, too, which obviously didn't go down well either. I'd like to apologise now to my classmates for any time I cost them during their education. I'm sorry.

Brilliantly, my mum and dad said that I should be entered for all eight O Levels. My dad even said that he would pay the entrance fees if the school wouldn't. The school relented – and, to their surprise, I passed all eight. So it was on to sixth form. In 1975, the grammar school was changing to a college and had its first intake of girls in the lower sixth. We couldn't believe our luck. But after five years at a boys' school we didn't know how to talk to them. I was too busy with sport that year anyway – I played for the school at football, rugby, cricket, basketball, badminton, table tennis and volleyball (my favourite). Mr Buck, the PE teacher, took me to play for Bracknell, who were in the first division at the time. I still love any sport.

I ended up with three A Levels in Geography, Maths (Pure and Statistics) and Biology – a D and two Es. I had wanted to go to Swansea to study Marine Geology (mainly because I'd learned to surf on the Gower the summer before), but unfortunately I didn't manage the two As and a B that they had offered. I was in America when the results came out, and then hitched down to Falmouth, so by the time I went to see the UCCA adviser there weren't many courses open to me.

My parents wanted me to study Geography but I wanted to do Drama. I explained this to the lady in an office just off Queensmead and she suggested I do both. We looked up Drama and Geography general degrees and two matches came up – York or Liverpool. Liverpool had the better football team so I signed up for Notre Dame, Liverpool. My mum and dad weren't happy, but they didn't try to stop me.

So that is how I ended up in Liverpool for six years. Very happy years they were, too. More of that later, because I want to get started on the journey. All you need to know for now is that I drifted through college and ended up failing my degree. I didn't hand in my dissertations until after the deadline and the college refused to accept them. I wasn't that bothered – I wasn't sure how having a piece of paper would help me become a comedian. But on results day I became a ghost. Everyone was celebrating except me. No one made eye contact. I went back to my room and let them get on with it. I didn't want to rain on their parade.

1

Leaving Liverpool

After failing my degree, I decided that I wanted to stay in Liverpool and repeat my final year. I intended doing it on the dole, taking the odd job here and there when my overdraft reached £100.

I managed to get a room in a house on Garmoyle Road with three girls – Rachel, Karen and Christine – who were two years below me at university. The house had no heating and that winter was a hard one. It was freezing! With very little money, I tended to spend the day under a pile of blankets and unzipped sleeping bags, and I'd have on all the clothes I owned. I had a 9-inch black and white TV to watch, but there were only three channels and there was nothing on in the mornings or afternoons, so I spent my time reading Russian literature and listening to Radio 4. I also started to write poetry. Bit of a cliché,

BOARD OF COLLEGE STUDIES
DEAN: C.H. CLOUGH, M.A., D.PHIL., F.R.HIST.S.
ADMINISTRATIVE SUB-DEAN: G. KELLY, B.SC. (ECON.), I.P.F.A., A.M.B.I.M.

19 ABERCROMBY SQUARE P.O. BOX 147 LIVERPOOL L69 3BX   TEL: 051 – 709 - 7312/3

The University of Liverpool

GK/CR   27th June 1980

Dear Mr. Smart,

   I am sorry to have to inform you that you have failed the B.A.
(general) degree examinations.

   If there are any reasons which may not have been known to the
Examiners and which may have contributed to your failure in the degree
examinations, you may ask to appear before the Progress Committee of
the Board of College Studies.   The Committee has no power to reverse
the Examiners' decision, but may decide that a candidate should be
permitted to repeat the third year with or without attendance.   Such a
recommendation will be made to the Senate only if new and telling evidence
is forthcoming; hence it will be in your own interests, if you decide to
appeal, to adduce as much evidence in support of it as you can.

   I should be grateful if you would let me have details of any appeal
as soon as possible.   If it is necessary for you to appear in person
before the Committee, you will be called for interview on Monday 21st
July.

                          Yours sincerely,

                          Graham Kelly
                          Administrative Sub-Dean

Mr. A.K. Smart,
Notre Dame College of Education.

wasn't I? But there were loads of us bohemians in any town or city with a university.

In the evenings I would meet up with friends in someone's kitchen. We had a copy of the *Pears' Cyclopaedia* and our favourite thing was to open it at any page and then ask a question from it. Whoever got the answer right asked the next question – we basically made our own quiz show. At 10 o'clock, we would walk round to The Brookhouse on Smithdown Road for a pint and then we'd head back to the house. At the weekend we would find a party to go to and on Saturdays we'd try to get to Anfield.

If Liverpool were playing at home when I was at uni, the two Geds – Smith and McCormack – and I would head down to Liverpool's A Division police station at about half past 10 on the Saturday morning. We would walk slowly up and down the street, then usually, at around 11, a policeman would come out and ask us if we would mind being in an identification parade. We would follow him into the station and into a grotty lime-green room, with a two-way mirror down one wall.

When the suspect was brought in, he was allowed to stand anywhere in the line he chose. We all stood very still and stared at the mirror in front of us. Occasionally the witness would come into the room with a police officer and was told to walk up and down the line and then to stand directly in front of the person they thought was the criminal. The strangest line-up we had was when a policeman came in and asked us to remove our shoes. 'Why?' we asked. 'Because the suspect has a lot of blood on his shoes,' replied the copper.

We had found out that you got £2 for a line-up, which paid for the bus trip to Anfield and for entrance to the ground, so once we had been paid we would head off to the game. It was a great time to be a Liverpool supporter in 1977: Kevin Keegan had just left and Kenny Dalgleish had arrived. It was a mix of the old and the new – Tommy Smith, Ian Callaghan, Jimmy Case and John Toshack from the Shankley era, then Emlyn Hughes, Alan Hansen, Phil Thompson, Graeme Souness and David Fairclough from the Paisley time. Liverpool won the European Cup that year and finished second to Brian Clough's Nottingham Forest team in the 1977–78 league.

Liverpool also beat Keegan's Hamburg team in the European Super Cup. The first leg was 1–1 in Hamburg and then the second leg was at Anfield on 6 December. We turned up to find the ground shrouded in fog, but Hamburg were keen to play rather than spend another night in Liverpool before their Saturday match back in Germany. It was one of the funniest nights I've ever had at a football game. Liverpool kicked off towards the Annie Road end and were 2–0 up at half-time, but no one in the crowd could see the other end of the pitch. When Liverpool came out for the second half, the Kop were ready. We had spent the first half singing:

Annie Road, tell us the score,

Tell us the score,

Tell us the score?

And they had kept us up to date with the goals. However, as soon as the game kicked off in the second half there was a Liverpool attack. A shot whistled past the post and went out for a goal kick. Conducted by a guy at the front of the terrace, the whole of the Kop cheered as one, with the supporters at the far end of the ground joining in. We kept this up for the whole 45 minutes. Liverpool ended up winning 6–0, but apparently the Annie Road end thought the score was 17–0.

The following March, Liverpool played Leeds United at home and beat them 1–0 with a goal from King Kenny. After the game, Ged McCormack and I didn't leave the ground – we waited in the toilets for about half an hour, then crept back onto the Kop. The ground was deserted and the floodlights were still on.

I'd picked up some discarded newspapers and had spent the time in the loo rolling them to a tight ball about the size of a grapefruit. Ged and I went down to the pitch and hopped over the waist-high wall onto the grass. I threw the paper ball onto the pitch and went in goal. Ged dribbled it back towards me, I dived over his shot, and it went into the net. The tannoy crackled to life: 'You boys! Go home now or there'll be trouble!' We ran back up the Kop, laughing, and out through the exit.

The following September, Tottenham were playing at Anfield. The term hadn't started but I'd gone back early. Pete Carey, my friend from Farnborough, was a Spurs fan and had come to visit. I told him we'd go to the match and stand on the famous Kop, but that he wasn't to talk as they would spot his accent and we might get some trouble.

After the sixth goal went in, the Kop started singing: 'Come on Tottenham. Come on Tottenham!' Pete joined in just a little too enthusiastically and soon the Scousers all round us were laughing and tousling his hair. Some of them apologised when Liverpool scored their last. In the end, Liverpool won 7–0 and Pete was heartbroken.

The Kop humour is legendary – we were forever laughing our way through a game – but my favourite song of all was when we played Manchester United. The week before the game it was announced in the newspapers that Tommy Docherty, their manager, had been having an affair with Mary Brown, the wife of the club's physio. It would eventually lead to his sacking and the start of the Alex Ferguson era (United fans should be very grateful to her), but he was still in charge for the Liverpool game. As he walked out of the tunnel on the halfway line and stepped onto the pitch, the Kop began to sing as if with one voice:

Who`s up Mary Brown,

Who`s up Mary Brown?

Bottom of the table you will go

E, I, E, I, E, I, O.

I was so lucky to spend those years in Liverpool, as that was probably the best team they have had in the last 50 years. The trophies speak for themselves: three League titles, two European Cups, two League Cups and that European Super Cup. I was very privileged to witness it.

I would occasionally go to lectures but my heart wasn't in studying – I was more into my own reading lists. I became obsessed with existentialism, reading everything I could: Sartre, Camus, Kafka, Burroughs, Melville. Bob Hornby, the drama lecturer, took a group of us to the Royal Exchange, Manchester, to see Trevor Peacock and Max Wall performing in *Waiting For Godot*. I was hooked on Beckett, so I decided to use my year to work towards a performance of *Krapp's Last Tape*, but I never did any of the exams and didn't bother handing in my thesis. Actually, I was the only student to achieve a Distinction for my live work.

For their final piece, Cathy Robinson and Rose Core wrote a play about Gertrude Stein and Alice B. Toklas during their spell in Paris in the 1920s. Brendan Routledge played Ernest Hemingway and I played F. Scott Fitzgerald and we talked in the play about a May spent in Biarritz. I loved the look of the word and promised myself I would go there one day.

In the afternoons I would head to the betting shop. I would place a 5p patent on three horses, so I'd get seven bets for 35p. I'd have a horse in the first race, one in the last race and one in-between so that I could stay in the shop all afternoon. They had radiators! I would study the form for ages, looking for trainers who were hot, and jockeys too. I preferred the jumps to the flat, but that might have been because I didn't need to keep warm in the summer. I became friendly with all the old boys who spent their afternoons in that smoky room. It wasn't like the banks of TVs you have now; there was a counter along the far wall as you came in, then down the right-hand wall was a blackboard where Terry wrote the results. Sometimes, when Terry didn't turn up, the bookie would let me write them up and I would be paid a pound when the shop shut at 5pm. I loved the atmosphere in there. There was a lot of laughter and discussions about all sorts of things – not just horses and dogs, but philosophy, politics and literature too.

I spent that summer watching the Ashes on a black and white telly at Matt Battersby's house. It was great to have the time to do this – and what a summer of cricket it was! Ian Botham in his pomp, Bob Willis charging in and Mike Brearley holding it all together.

I had moved out of the Garmoyle Road house in June and had begun three months of sofa surfing – starting with another house on Garmoyle Road shared by Steve, Dean and Tony. It was a crazy house! One weekend I hitched down to see my girlfriend Julie in Bristol. When I returned on the Monday, I found that the living-room floor was now three feet lower than when I had left. The boys didn't tell me about this – I found out by opening the door and falling into the rubble that had once been the floor. It turned out that they had held a party on the Saturday, inviting everyone back from The Brookhouse. Hearing the party, more and more people had come in. My bedroom – the living room – had turned into a dance room, but the floorboards were obviously rotten and the whole crowd had suddenly dropped.

My next home was thanks to Moira Fogg. She was dating an architect, Tony Flannery, who lived with another architect, Mike, just round the corner. (Moira and Tony later married and are now living in Auckland, New Zealand.) They were great fun. Mike was always going on about painting the kitchen, so, on his birthday, Tony and I wrote 'HAPPY BIRTHDAY MIKE!' in big letters with a six-inch brush, all round the walls. It was still there at his following birthday.

In September, two girls from college came to the door with a cardboard box containing a black kitten. They had tried to keep it at the halls of residence but the nuns had a 'no pets' rule, so they brought it to us to look after for them. They promised to visit it every day and said they would feed it, but we didn't see them for four days after that. When they did turn up, they asked us what we had called the kitten. To be honest, we hadn't given it a thought as we still considered it to be their cat. They couldn't believe it and said, 'You have to name him today.' Tony and I looked at each other mischievously and said, 'OK.'

From then on, the cat was called Today. The joke backfired on us, though. When you wanted him to come into the house at bedtime, you had to stand at the kitchen door shouting, 'Today! Come here, Today!'

One of Mike's projects for his master's degree was a study of Norman Foster and his glass exteriors on buildings. Foster had developed a new way of fixing panes of glass together using a metal clamp with four short arms and Mike needed a photo of one of these clamps. So he paid me £20 to hitch to Swindon, where there was a new factory being built on an industrial estate. It was the first time this process had been used and so this was the only place in the country where I could get the photo. Armed with Mike's camera, I set off at six the next morning. I hitched down the M6, then the M5 to Bristol, and then I cut across on the M4 to Swindon. I walked from the motorway turn-off to the factory, getting there at 1pm. Mike had warned me that they might not like me taking photos, but I had worked on a couple of building sites before, thanks to my dad, so I just walked onto the site and grabbed a hard hat from outside the tea shed. I found one of the clamps at eye level on one of the building's corners. I took out the camera and got a few snaps, put it back in the bag and headed off the site, placing the hard hat back on the bench as I left.

I managed to catch a lift in a lorry from the industrial park to Cheltenham and then another up the M5 to Keele services. From there I got a lift in a car to Warrington, where I hopped on a bus back to Liverpool. Mike was very surprised to see me back by seven that evening but he was thrilled with the snaps I had taken.

The next day was 23 December, and I was back on the road. This time I was hitching to Knutsford to see Julie – it was annoying because she couldn't leave until the next day. She was studying to be a vet at Bristol University but for part of her course she had to spend time on different farms for three weeks at a time. She'd already done a chicken farm and a stud farm, and her third was a dairy farm which was adjacent to Knutsford services on the M6. It was bitterly cold as I caught the bus to the start of the East Lancs Road that afternoon. The first car (a guy going to London for Christmas) stopped after five minutes waiting – sometimes it just happened like that. I jumped out at Knutsford and walked round to the farm, where the farmer didn't seem that happy to see me.

'Where's he going to sleep?' he asked angrily.

'With me,' Julie replied.

'Not in my house,' came the retort. 'He can have the sofa down here.'

'OK, that's great,' I said, planning all the while to creep up to Julie's room as soon as he was asleep.

'We've got no food for him either,' said the farmer, full of the Christmas spirit.

'We'll get something at the pub, then,' said Julie, fetching her coat from the rack and marching me out of the door.

We walked to the pub and had a few pints and some good pub food thanks to Mike's 20 quid note. Then we headed back to the house with a bottle of wine. As we walked, great big flakes of snow began to fall. It was very romantic. The farmer was on his way up to bed and as he climbed the stairs he reminded Julie that morning milking was at 5.30. We put the TV on. *The Man Who Fell To Earth* was just starting, so we opened the wine and sat in front of the roaring fire under a rug. At one point the farmer came down for a glass of water (to check on us more like!) and told us we were degenerates for watching a David Bowie film. Anyway, we turned off the telly at midnight and kissed and cuddled for a bit as Julie was worried we would be heard if we went upstairs. With the warmth of the fire and the alcohol, we must have drifted off in each other's arms on the couch.

I was woken at 5am by the farmer, who was standing over me and shouting at me to get my stuff. I informed him that nothing was going on – we both still had all our clothes on.

He said, 'Good! Now get all your warm clothes on. What size wellies do you take?'

'Huh?' I spluttered. 'Elevens.'

He ran into the kitchen as I put on lots of layers. He returned with a mud-spattered pair of wellies and threw them at me.

'What's going on?' I enquired.

'Heavy snow. I need you to help me find the cows.'

Two feet of snow had fallen in the night. The cows had lain down and were now completely covered, some in deep drifts that the wind had formed. He sent Julie to the milking shed with a load of dirty blankets to wipe down the cows as we freed them. It was hard work. For a start it was pitch black, with dark snow clouds covering the moon. The only light came from the service station a mile away. He gave me a torch and a six-foot pole and we headed to the field the cows were in.

There were 28 cows to find but I couldn't see even one when we arrived at the gate. The snow was ball-deep and I was already frozen. We walked around, gently pushing our poles into the snow where it was deeper than in the rest of the field. If the pole hit something soft, you had a cow. You had to shovel the snow off it with your hands, working towards the head, then you had to urge the cow to stand up and lead it back to the milking shed, where Julie would take care of it. It was quite alarming when they stood up out of the snow in the torchlight.

Some freed themselves when they heard us and eventually went back to the milking shed by themselves, following the tracks of those before them. It took three hours to find them all. The last two were the hardest to find – they were at the bottom of the field against the fence, where the snow was deepest. Eventually we found them and dug them out. My hands and feet were frozen. Once we had milked them, we headed back to the farmhouse, where the farmer's wife cooked us an amazing full English breakfast.

As we ate, the farmer apologised for his original reaction to me. He thanked me effusively, as he'd been sure he was going to lose some animals that morning. He thanked Julie too and asked her how we were getting back to Farnborough, where we both came from. When she explained that we were hitching he would have none of it. He drove us to Knutsford and bought us two train tickets to London for helping him out. Unfortunately, the snow had made a lot of people change their travel plans and the train was very overcrowded – we had to sit in a corridor on our bags for the six-hour journey back to Euston.

One of the craziest journeys that I hitched involved a bet. A stupid bet. A bet born from boredom and a lack of pennies in my pocket to buy the next round. I was living on the dole at the time, so we didn't have much money, but we made our own fun. The lack of jobs and the overzealous use of the 'sus' law by the police had caused the riots a couple of months earlier that summer.

One night, in September, I sat in a pub on Lark Lane with five friends, making each pint last an hour. The previous weekend I had hitched to London for a birthday party on the Saturday, and back on the Sunday. I was bragging about how easy it had been and how I could get everywhere quickly, and we started talking about how far I could get in a day. Someone said, 'How about Inverness?' I thought that was possible. Then someone else said, 'How about to the top of Ben Nevis?' We all laughed. But I considered it and then said, 'I bet I can get to the top of Ben Nevis and back in 48 hours.' There was a checking of pockets. Everyone put £2 in a pint glass and the bet was on.

'When do you want me to do it?' I asked. One of them looked at the clock; it was 10pm. 'How about now?' he said. I laughed and then realised they were being serious. They emptied my pockets to make sure that I didn't have any money to pay for transport, though I was allowed to keep 60p for food. Then I ran out of the pub and caught a bus to the East Lancs Road.

I hitched through the night, arriving in Glasgow at about 10am. I was dropped in the centre and it took a while to walk to the A82, the road to Oban. I finally reached Fort William at three that afternoon. I went into the information centre and asked how long it took to climb Ben Nevis. The woman thought for a minute and said, 'About seven hours.' Ah, I thought, that's buggered it. 'So you wouldn't advise anyone to start out now?' I posed. 'It'll be dark by eight and you've got to get back down too.'

I walked outside and across to a shingle beach. I couldn't wait until tomorrow or I wouldn't make it back in time. I looked up at Ben Nevis, its top shrouded in grey clouds. Sod it, I thought. Let's give it a go. I dipped my hand in the sea so I could go from sea level to 4,413 feet in one, and ran off down the road.

The first couple of miles are on tarmac and farm tracks and I made good time, but then the climb started. As I ran, jumped and leapt up the path, I met quite a few people coming down the mountain. After three and a half hours, I'd reached the summit. The last

2,000 feet of track had been through a swirling fog caused by the low cloud level; visibility became very poor and I started to panic.

The boys had given me a disposable camera from behind the bar in the pub and I had to take a photo by the trig point that marks the highest part of the mountain. Eventually, I found it. Now I needed to find someone to take the photo, as this was 30 years before selfies. I stood shouting in the mist for five minutes before, literally, bumping into a Canadian couple, who told me that they had left their B&B at nine that morning. They took a couple of photos – although when they were developed, it looked like I was standing in a sauna. I thanked them and headed off back down.

Running down Ben Nevis that evening, in the worsening light, was one of the most exhilarating things I've ever done. It took a lot of concentration, and sure feet, but I was flying. The views were stunning, when I dared to look up. It took me an hour and a half to get down. I was covered in sweat, hungry and thirsty, but I had to start hitching back.

My first lift took me to Oban and I was a little overconfident that I'd arrive back way before the deadline. Oban is in a beautiful setting between the mountains and the sea but it isn't very big and there wasn't much traffic. I walked back to a chip shop I'd passed and got a bag of chips. Back at the edge of town there was now no traffic at all. Eventually a lorry appeared and I not only put out my thumb but waved frantically too, and then put my hands in the prayer position. He stopped. He'd just come down from Fort William (dagnabbit!). That lift got me as far as Glasgow – but it was the wrong side of Glasgow, so I traipsed through the city to the centre and spent the last of my money on a bus to the M77.

The sun was coming up and I needed to sleep, but it took three hours to catch the next lift. I put it down to people being grumpy, or late, at that time of the morning. Eventually, I caught one to just outside Carlisle, but I then had another long wait before moving on to Kendal services, in the Lake District. It was now 3pm and I was struggling – struggling with time, struggling with lack of sleep, and I was desperately hungry. I waited at the exit but no one wanted to give me a lift, probably because I looked a bit mad.

I decided something had to be done. So I walked into the services to the area where people were eating, stood on a chair and said in a loud voice, 'Hi, this is going to sound weird but I bet my mates, two days ago, that I could hitch from Liverpool to Ben Nevis, climb it and then get back to Liverpool by 10 o'clock tonight. I beseech you, ladies and gentlemen, if anyone can give me a lift in that direction, I'd be very grateful.' I'd lost most of them after 'Hi', but one guy in a suit came over. He worked for a glass manufacturer and said he'd get me to St Helens.

After hearing my story, he told me to get some sleep and the next thing I knew we were parked on the slip road from the East Lancs Road, by St Helens. I asked him what time it was and he said it was 7.30. What a star! I covered the last 15 miles to Liverpool city centre in three-quarters of an hour and then walked the last couple of miles to Aigburth. I reached the pub by 9.15, but I didn't go in. No, I waited until 9.50 and then charged in laughing, to be met by a lot of swearing. When the photos were developed, there were a few heated arguments, but I had in my pocket a map from the information centre in Fort William, which they couldn't argue with.

Eventually I got a flat of my own on Princes Avenue in Toxteth. The rent was £7 a week. The reason for moving out of Mike and Tony's flat was that I had got a job with a TiE (Theatre in Education) company called 489, initially as a writer.

Throughout the winter I had been performing every week on a Monday in the basement of the Casablanca Club – the 'Casa' – on Hope Street, a notorious joint between Liverpool's two cathedrals. The Poetry and Folk Club was a very friendly event run by an old hippy who would always sing Neil Young's 'Hey Hey, My My' plaintively with all of his soul. I loved it – I wish I had a recording. I would get up and read my poems each week, and in the end I would compère the gig (my pay was three bottles of lager). I would try to write a half-hour's worth of new poems each week, but sometimes I would turn to a blank page in my notebook without letting the audience see and then I would just make up a poem. I suppose it was my first experience of improvising in front of an audience.

One night Albie Donnelly from the band Supercharge came in. I had been to see the poet Adrian Henri the week before and had been less than impressed with his poem about New York, which I thought was a poor imitation of an Allen Ginsberg poem, so I had written a poem imitating Henri imitating Ginsberg. Albie loved it and asked me if I would read it at the band's Christmas show in the basement of the Everyman Theatre. It was on 28 December and I hitch-hiked back to Liverpool from my mum and dad's that day. I was shaking with nerves the whole of the journey.

This would be the biggest audience I had performed for professionally, as I was to be paid a fiver. My first paid gig. Albie told me I'd be going on at the start of the second half with another poet – a 16-year-old called Craig Charles. It was also his first ever gig. What he didn't tell me was that he had invited Adrian Henri along. I spotted him and his photographer girlfriend standing at the back halfway through my piss-take.

I finished reading it, but I was the colour of a Santa Claus who'd sat too near the fire.

After the show at the Casa I would hang out with the other bohemians who frequented the place. On the ground floor there were two rooms. One was a bar, which had a couple of optics and a fridge full of Red Stripe. The other side of the long hall was a large room, like a sitting room with no furniture. They didn't want to pay a DJ, so they had a juke box in the bay window. It had some great tunes on it: ska, reggae, punk and soul. At the end of the hall was a staircase up to private rooms where, rumour had it, all sorts went on.

There was a police raid every month. If I was on stage at the time (it happened twice), I would calmly say over the mike, 'Don't go to the loos to flush your drugs as there is a plain-clothes policeman waiting in there.' It was strange the police always chose a Monday to raid the place, as it was pretty empty on Mondays. They never seemed to raid at the weekends.

This was the height of bad feeling towards the police in Liverpool. The government had brought in the 'sus' law enabling the police to stop and search anyone. They seemed to be biased in those they stopped, though. In Toxteth, where the unemployment rate was running at 45 per cent at the time, the population was predominantly black. Late at night it felt like walking through a war zone. Eventually it had to happen; after a lock-in at the Casa I set off to walk the half-mile to my flat at around half past one in the morning. I was weaving a bit when a panda car pulled up alongside me and two coppers jumped out. They started questioning me as to what I was doing walking around Toxteth at that time of night. I'd seen 'stop and search' many times in the area, and asked them, 'Why are you stopping me? Don't you usually only stop black kids?' They didn't like this for some reason and pushed me into the car and drove me back to the police station. I was marched to the desk sergeant and quizzed again as to why I was walking round Toxteth at that time of night.

'Because I live here,' I replied.

'Where's that, then, sonny?'

'Princes Park Avenue,' I said with pride.

'And where are you coming from then?'

'The Casablanca Club.'

'And what have you been doing there exactly?'

'Poetry.'

The word had a magic effect. The entrance room at Toxteth police station was quite a large area, with two fake-leather sofas that had seen better days. Around these were plastic chairs screwed to the floor. Sitting on these were assorted hard men, drug dealers and pimps. At the word 'poetry' they had all stopped what they were doing and began earwigging the conversation between myself and the desk sergeant.

'Poetry?' came his reply.

'Er, yes. I'm the resident poet there.'

'And I suppose you have some poems with you, to substantiate this claim?' he asked.

'Um, yes.'

'Well, I guess we should hear them, then,' he said, with a twinkle in his eye.

'What, now?' I gulped, looking round at the assembled company.

'No, not yet,' he chuckled. 'Let me get the lads out of the canteen first. I'm sure they would love to hear some poetry at this point on the shift. You see, we don't get many poets in here.'

He left to fetch his mates and I looked through the pages in my pocket for a suitable poem. I stood in front of the double doors and waited. The crowd were waiting too. They hadn't been expecting this, their faces told me. Most of them wore huge smiles as I stood there blushing in my duffel coat.

The canteen emptied and joined the throng. I have had tough audiences since then (including the Meccano Club on 5 November 1996, when I asked all 28 of them outside for a fight), but none tougher than that night.

I mumbled and stumbled through the first poem to complete silence. Then looked up expectantly.

'Do another one,' said the desk sergeant.

I searched through the bits of paper and found a prose poem about walking across Sefton Park, at night, after leaving a lover's bed.

A couple of the civilians were now offering smiles of encouragement. But not the police. When I finished, one bloke clapped. But everyone swung round to stare at him and he soon stopped.

'That's enough, lad.'

'Can I go now?' I asked, with a quiver in my voice.

'Go on then,' came the reply.

I turned and walked out the door. As it closed behind me I heard the roar of laughter from the assembled crowd.

July 1981 was hot. It had been hot for weeks. Tensions between the local community and the police were running high. On 3 July the police arrested Leroy Cooper after stopping him on sus. A crowd had gathered to watch and they turned nasty when they perceived that the police were being heavy handed. A scuffle broke out and three policemen were injured. Over the weekend the disturbance turned into full-scale rioting. There were petrol bombs and everything.

I lived about 200 yards from where it started and my first-floor flat had a grandstand view of events. I lived opposite The Silver Sands nightclub, one of five bars in the basements of the Victorian buildings that lined the road. The Sands, as we used to call it, seemed to be the hub of the riots. There were no mobile phones in those days, obviously, so 16-year old lads on mopeds came and went through day and night, telling those inside where the police were gathering and allowing the rioters to stay one step ahead. Coppers were being brought in from all over the country, but they were disadvantaged as they didn't know the area.

On the Sunday night, the mob attacked the Racquets Club, an old building from the days when Liverpool was a successful port. Just three months before, I had paid a pound to watch Omar Sharif play backgammon there. Most of the police had been moved to Smithdown Road to deal with a large crowd and the building didn't stand a chance. Soon it was on fire. As the blaze intensified the police regrouped and fired tear gas into the crowd, who started to run back down Princes Park Avenue.

I was sitting at my open window and heard them before I saw them. As they ran down the street with the police in pursuit, some were knocking on doors, shouting for refuge. I ran downstairs and shouted to the nearest group. The next thing I knew I had about 30 people in my one-room flat. Everyone was thanking me profusely. Those who had been in contact with the gas were taken into the bathroom and given eyewashes. After about two or three hours, the police had moved on and people drifted away, heading home.

The next morning I went to get the papers from the local shop on Granby Street. There was broken glass and bricks littered all over the road. Toxteth was a very poor area; large swathes of terraced houses had been cleared after the war and the ground had never been built on. There was plenty of ammo for the rioters.

I reached the shop, but found it shut. There was a police cordon around Toxteth that morning and the shop owner hadn't made it through yet. As I stood around wondering what to do next, a van came hurtling down the road. It screamed to a halt next to me, then the driver threw it into reverse, mounted the kerb and backed into the shop front. There was a loud crash as the window smashed and fell to the pavement. The back doors of the van opened and four blokes in balaclavas jumped out and started throwing anything they could get their hands on into the back of the van, including the till. Then they slammed the doors shut, the van shot off towards the park and the four guys ran off towards the city.

The whole enterprise took about 30 seconds. I stood there gobsmacked. This was my local shop. Why were they attacking their own? I was all for rioting against police brutality, but this crossed the line.

As I stood there, open-mouthed, an old lady came past with her grandson. 'Quick!' she said to the boy.

'Get me some fags!' The boy looked around the street, then darted into the broken shop, returning with two cartons (40 packs) of Silk Cut.

'NO!' she shouted, cuffing him round the ear. 'Not those! You know I only smoke Player's.'

The boy jumped back into the shop, threw down the Silk Cut and grabbed two cartons of Player's No. 6. She hurriedly stuffed the fags into her shopping trolley and they continued on their way.

I headed back to my flat, although I did go back a couple of days later to give the owner a statement for his insurance claim. As I crossed Mulgrave Street, I couldn't believe my eyes. Parked in the middle of the road, amidst the detritus of the previous nights' rioting, was a large black Bentley, with a flag on its bonnet. I went to see what was happening. It was the Lord Mayor of Liverpool. Such insensitivity. He stood there in his gold chains of office in front of his flash motor, shaking hands with local business people. He just didn't get it. This privilege was what the riots were about. I fear we are returning to such days now.

Paul, who ran the TiE company, had also been in to see the poetry club, so when I turned up for the audition he knew who I was. I was taken on as a writer, but that meant I was left in the office while the actors went around the local schools performing. So I started to write more parts than there were actors, so they had to put me in the shows too. I wrote *Alice and the Bee*, a play about conservation, for seven-year-olds. *Not a Penny off the Pay* was about the 1926 General Strike, and *Billy's Crash*, for sixth-formers, was about disability.

In the first show, *Alice and the Bee*, I played a nasty wasp, henchman to the wicked queen. We toured it in November and December 1981 – it was almost like a panto that came to your school. As Christmas approached we were pretty comfortable with the show. And some headteachers would even offer us a mince pie and a sherry.

Usually, we did one school in the morning, then put the two flats with the scenery in the back of the van, and the giant tape player too. Then it was off to the afternoon school via a pub for lunch, and back to the storage lock-up in the evening. Then they added an extra show a day, so we'd turn up at the first school at nine, do the show, pack everything into the van and head off to the next one. Same again and into the nearest pub. We didn't have time to get changed between the shows, so it must have looked weird when a schoolgirl, a cat, a wasp, a witch and a bee walked into those boozers in Huyton and Bootle. The third show of the day was hysterical. Goodness only knows what those kids thought of it.

The girl playing the witch didn't come on during the first half, but there was a lot of talk about how horrible she was. Eventually she would hurtle out from behind the scenery and charge down the hall/dining room towards the kids seated on the floor. She would be laughing maniacally, louder and louder, and then she'd lower her head and softly hiss, 'Hello, my pretties.' We used to have a sweepstake on how many kids would need to be taken out because they started crying or pissed themselves.

One afternoon we arrived straight from the pub to be met by a headmistress with a tray of sherry. We'd already had a couple in each of the first two schools and then two pints in the pub, and this last sherry pushed the witch over the edge. She decided to really go for it. Her crazed laugh started behind the screen and grew louder and louder. Then she appeared, running really fast, her arms flailing and her head whipping round all over the place. She did a circuit of the hall like this before running straight at the kids. But when she tried to stop she hit a puddle of wee that one of the kids had let out in fear. She slid through the piss and the front three rows, cracking her head as she went down. There was a lot of crying from the kids. The bee and the cat carried the wicked witch offstage and I stepped in. I calmed the kids down somehow – not easy when you are dressed as a giant wasp – and got them to cheer loudly for themselves.

I said, 'Go on, give yourselves a cheer. We've been to about 50 schools and you are the first one to beat the wicked witch at this point of the show. Let's sing some carols.'

Not a Penny off the Pay was a more ambitious show. We split the kids into three groups: the mine owners, the shop owners and villagers, and the miners. We would build a mine out of blankets and chairs, too. In the first half of the show we told each of the groups how their lives would have been in 1926 and then in the second half they would act them out. So the miners would work down the mine, earn money and then give it to the shop owners in exchange for food and fuel. The shop owners and the villagers would spend it. The mine owners had hunting trips and board meetings. Being a southerner, I led the mine owners.

Everything went well for about 20 minutes until the mine owners were told that the price of coal had gone down and they could either cut the upcoming safety work or take a penny off the miners' pay. At one school, they decided to do both. Life in the village would break down. We would steer the whole piece towards a strike and the mine owners were usually forced to climb down. But we didn't really mind where we ended up.

My favourite outcome came at a school in Huyton. The miners formed a union and sent their representative to talk to the mine owners. He was a brilliant little boy who spoke eloquently about how the mine needed better safety conditions and how the miners, rather than be docked pay, should get more, as there would still be enough money for the owners to live on comfortably. A socialist dream. I looked at the other mine owners; they were not for turning. So the young lad said to me, 'Please come down the mine. I'll show you the poor working conditions.'

Playing along, I went with him and crawled along the tunnel we'd built, 30 feet to the end. There was a group of kids waiting, and as soon as I was scrunched in they fell on top of me and told me I was their hostage. I had to laugh. Socialism to terrorism in one step. But we had always said that we had to be true to the piece and stay in character until we left the building. Pretentious, I know. So I played along. A miner was sent to the surface to tell them what was happening. It was hilarious. It took a full hour of negotiations to get me out, and we had to miss the lunchtime pint. But we all agreed the kids had been brilliant. The miners got their way, too!

Billy's Crash was for sixth-formers and was the show I'm most proud of. It was written for the Year of the Disabled and told the story of a young scally who takes the mickey out of the disabled and calls his best mate (played by me) a 'spacky' because he's a bit slow. But then he steals a car and is chased by the police. There is a car crash and he is left paralysed from the waist down.

Once Billy sees life from the other perspective, he realises the error of his ways. When he woke up in hospital after the crash we would play Pink Floyd's 'Comfortably Numb', as Billy gradually realised where he was. It was very moving. There would always be a few students crying.

To understand life with a disability we spent a week exploring the parameters placed on the disabled. A day was spent blindfolded, being led round Church Street and other shopping streets in Liverpool city centre, and then the next day we had to wear earplugs all day. We also spent three days in wheelchairs, finding out how inaccessible shops, pubs and public buildings were. There were three disabled people in chairs with us and they would point out their problems. We became quite good at wheelies, which you need to do to get up a high step. There were races, too – the disabled people always won. Sometimes they hung back in a race and tried to come alongside us and crush our fingers between the wheels. It was very *Ben-Hur*.

We became very close and, after three days, they suggested a night out. We said we'd have to take the chairs back, but they suggested that we continue in them. So off we rolled. After six or seven pints, one of the girls in a wheelchair said, 'Let's go to a nightclub!' They said they knew of one close by that was wheelchair-friendly. We finished our pints and followed them down a side street. We came to the door of a club where the bouncers obviously knew our new-found friends and waved us in. But they had omitted to tell us that the club was in a basement. Paul, another actor, looked at me, fear in his eyes. I was sobering up rapidly. What would these two bruisers think if we stood up and walked down the stairs? The disabled guys enjoyed our discomfort immensely as the two bouncers carried us down the stairs one at a time. Once we were down there, the club was brilliant. People made space for us by the bar, as buying drinks from a wheelchair is incredibly difficult. By the end of the night, we were all on the dancefloor doing spins and wheelies in time to the music. The bouncers carried us all back to the street and we pushed ourselves drunkenly back to the van. I never went back to that club, ever.

The TiE team was led by Paul, who was going out with team member number two, Helen. There was Gill, who did all the admin and also performed in the show; Michelle, who everybody called Micky; Pauline, a petite actress; and lastly there was Ian. Ian was from Ormskirk, a gentle man who loved Irish wolfhounds. It was Ian who taught me to juggle. Thank you, Ian! If he hadn't, I wouldn't have had the career that I've had.

Sadly, I had fallen for Helen, but she was in love with Paul. I realised that living with this unrequited love was making me sad – very sad – and I wanted a change. I wanted another trip round Europe. It was the summer of 1982. There was a World Cup about to start in Spain, and England were playing France in Bilbao on my birthday. So I quit my job, put everything I would need in my trusty red rucksack and gave everything else away to friends. I gave back the keys to my flat at 8pm on 31 May and caught the bus to the start of the East Lancs Road. It felt important. As I stood there, I realised it was the end of my time in Liverpool. A new beginning. I didn't realise that it would shape my life forever, but it did. I was on my way. I would head to Portsmouth and then on to France and Spain.

2

Stoke

As I stood watching the sun setting over the city, I wondered what the next month would hold. There is no way I could have predicted the first lift of the journey: after about 10 minutes of waiting, a rust bucket of a small van pulled up. I ran to the passenger window and, as it opened, a cloud of dope smoke flowed out, nearly knocking me over. There were two lads of 18 in the seats at the front and a 16-year-old boy standing in the back, his head between the other two.

'Where are you headed?' I asked.

'Stoke,' replied the driver.

'Great.'

We then stood staring at each other. Eventually the penny dropped and the guy in the passenger seat got in the back with my rucksack, I took his seat, and we started. The car was extremely slow to go through the gears – it took about five miles to reach fourth, which meant that the car was at maximum velocity. The driver reached down between his legs and grabbed a breeze block, placed it on the accelerator and then sat back and put both feet on the dashboard.

It was one of the most frightening lifts of my life. The driver was stoned but the other two had taken speed as well, which meant that the two in the back wouldn't stop talking and the driver wasn't concentrating on the road. They asked me where I was going. When I told them I was off to the World Cup, they started singing football songs. As we turned onto the M6 they rolled another spliff. They were headed to Stoke for an all-nighter at some club and tried to convince me to go with them, but I jumped out on the slip road, thankful that I was still alive.

I knew this bit of the motorway network very well. After my third year at college, my girlfriend at the time, Stephanie, had taken a job as a primary-school teacher in Ashbourne in Derbyshire. I had tried to hitch down to see her every Friday, returning on Monday morning, so I grew to know people who travelled that route regularly at those times and could do it in two hours each way. After her first month there, I received a letter from Stephanie saying that she was unhappy and homesick for Liverpool; she said the only thing she had to look forward to was a trip to Nottingham Playhouse on the Thursday. There were no mobiles in those days – in fact, there was no phone at all at the lodging house where she was living. So the next day – Thursday – I got up early and hitched to Nottingham. I wanted to surprise her and give her a lift, as it were, but the journey took forever and by the time I arrived the play had started. I sat in the foyer and waited. The interval came and Stephanie appeared in the middle of a group of middle-aged women. She was shocked to see me. I had bought some flowers at a service station and presented them to her.

'I've come to cheer you up!' I said with a big grin.

'Why?' asked Steph.

'Your letter.'

'Oh, that. Well, I wrote that on Sunday. I'm all right now.'

This wasn't going how I'd planned. 'Um, oh, OK. Well, can I come back to Ashbourne with you?'

'Sorry, no. My landlady doesn't allow gentlemen visitors.'

'Don't worry – I'm not a gentleman!'

'And there's no room in the minibus.'

'OK.'

The bell went for the start of the second half, she gave me a peck on the cheek, and I left. I hitched all night to get home – in fact, I travelled for 25 hours for a peck on the cheek.

That February I was introduced to a game that I have followed ever since: the Royal Shrovetide Football at Ashbourne (there's a game on Shrove Tuesday and also one on Ash Wednesday every year). If you ever get the chance to see it, jump at it — it's a fantastic day's entertainment. It's basically a game of football as played in the 17th century. The goals are three miles apart at either end of the town and the teams are made up of roughly 300 a side — those born south of the Henmore Brook play for the Down'Ards and those to the north for the Up'Ards. The ball is made of solid cork, covered in hand-painted leather, and is the size of a medicine ball. Whoever scores a goal gets to keep the ball, which can be worth £1,000. To score a goal, a player must jump into the river and bang the ball three times on a millstone embedded in the bank. The ball gets 'turned up' at 2pm in the car park in the centre of town, and if a goal is scored before 5pm another is released. If there is no score by 10pm, the police take custody of the ball and it is a draw.

The game has only three rules:

1. The hug (a sort of huge rugby scrum) must not enter the churchyard, the Memorial Gardens, or the gardens of houses.
2. No murder.

3. The ball must not be carried on any form
of transport.

This last rule came about after two incidents. First,
the ball was thrown through the open window of
a train carriage pulling out of the station. The man
who planned it then pulled the emergency cord and
stopped the train near the goal, jumped down and
ran across the fields to score unopposed. The second
incident happened in the 1950s, when someone threw
the ball to the pillion rider on a motorbike and off
they went to score.

The year I played my first game for the Down'Ards.
I dressed in old clothes – boots, tracksuit bottoms, two
T-shirts and a big jumper. It was cold, with snow on
the ground. We went in Henmore Brook twice, and
the water was freezing. It wasn't until about five games
later that some of the other players admitted they wore
a wet suit under their clothes.

We headed down to the town and had a few pints
in The Horns. In those days they threw the ball up
from some steps across the road from The Green Man.
After we had sung the national anthem and 'Auld
Lang Syne', the ball was thrown into the waiting
crowd on the road. Suddenly there was an outbreak of
madness, both teams crowding in to get round the ball
in the hug. The crowd is like a giant amoeba in the
way it moves, but when one side gets going it can be
quite fast. If the ball gets stuck in one spot for a while,

a favourite tactic is to force it up above the heads of the hug and to bat it in the direction you want it to go. There are runners at the edge of the hug waiting for moments like these. If they can grab hold of the ball, they're off.

All the buildings and shops are boarded up for the games. There's a great story that one year in the early 1970s, a new manager who had just been installed in Woolworth's said the staff had to work the two days as there would be a lot of people in town. This was unheard of. Everyone takes the day off, except the pubs, which make an absolute fortune – it's very thirsty work pushing and shoving for up to eight hours. Anyway, he didn't put the boards up over the doors. The hug somehow ended up outside and was gleefully pushed through the store, right down the centre aisle and out through the back door. It did about £2,000 worth of damage. Needless to say, the manager was sacked and the shop workers had the day off the following year.

The hug went through the town and into residential streets. At one point we went through someone's hedge and into their garden, so the stewards called a halt and everyone moved back into the middle of the road. Some players knocked on the door to take down the owner's details so they could come back at the weekend to repair any damage. I remember getting crushed against the side of a car just after this and I couldn't get my breath. When the hug moved on I collapsed to the ground, gasping for air. There were cries of 'Man down!' and suddenly a dozen hands reached down as the crowd stepped back and I was hauled to my feet.

At that time, Ashbourne had the most pubs per head of population in the whole country, so every hour or so we would dash into the nearest one and have a pint. Then, when we came out, we would ask a policeman where the ball was (the police had walkie-talkies and could check). We would hare off in pursuit of the ball and rejoin the hug. When it got dark we were up on the sports fields of the grammar school – there were puddles and hedges, small copses and the river to deal with. Players would start false balls, to take players away from the real one – there was a lot of confusion.

I played that day until 9pm, when a goal was scored by one G. Harrison for the Up'Ards. In seven hours I had touched the ball five times. I was terribly deflated to be on the losing side – everyone puts so much effort into the game. I must have played in over 20 games now and for the last eight years I have reported on it for the Hawksbee and Jacobs show on TalkSport, commentating while playing.

I finished with Steph on her birthday. She had a party and I hitched down to see her. It was hard keeping up a long-distance relationship and it turned out she had been seeing her neighbour in the flats where she lived. I was angry more than heartbroken. It was pride, I guess – all her friends seemed to know about it. I said I wanted to sleep and that I would leave first thing in the morning. She asked her new bloke for his keys and I went next door with half a bottle of whisky and passed out. I awoke at six and decided to head off, but when I left the flats I found that there had been a snowstorm in the night. It was waist-deep at points and I wasn't dressed for it, but I couldn't go back in. So I waded through the drifts, across the town and out to the start of the A52, which took me an hour. There was a pub there in those days and the landlord was just getting up. He saw me through the window as I stared up at the hill out of town, completely blocked by snow.

'You won't be going nowhere till the snow plough comes,' the landlord shouted from his front door. 'Come in and have a cup of tea. You look flipping frozen!'

So that is what I did. He made me a lovely fry-up and I warmed my hands on the mug of tea. At about eight, the snow plough came slowly down the hill and turned in front of the pub. I thanked the innkeeper and ran out of the door, holding my thumb out in front of the snow drift on the left-hand side of the road that was still to be cleared. To my great surprise, the driver stopped and beckoned me to climb up into the cab. It was brilliant – the great plough on the front sent up a wall of snow into the adjacent fields as we drove along. Halfway to Leek we reached the Derbyshire–Staffordshire border. The road ahead was clear, so the driver told me he was heading back to Ashbourne. I thanked him profusely and leapt down from the truck. He turned round and drove off. I put my thumb out.

Each car stopped to ask where I was going. They had seen me climb down from the snow plough and wanted to reward me for the job I'd done. The fifth car was going to Liverpool and I was back in my flat by lunchtime. I didn't tell the guy who gave me the lift that I had nothing to do with the snow plough, but I was always making stuff up anyway. I figured I'd never see these people again, so I could be anyone I wanted to be. I did so much hitching in those years that I got quite bored of telling people the same story over and over again. So sometimes I would tell them I was a dry-stone-wall builder and sometimes it was a mole catcher. Another favourite was coastguard. In a way, it must have helped with the improvisation skills that I still use to this day with The Comedy Store Players at The Comedy Store every Wednesday and Sunday.

I spent a lot of time in the autumn and winter of 1980–81 hitching around the Midlands. One of the strangest lifts I ever had was from Leicester to Coventry. It was a hot day, and I had been waiting nearly an hour for a lift. Then a lorry stopped – a massive artic – and I ran down the slip road and climbed in. The driver was a small chubby man wearing what looked like a woman's blouse. I didn't say anything. We pulled onto the motorway, making small talk for a while about the weather. I kept looking at him out of the corner of my eye. Something wasn't quite right here. He caught me looking at him.

'Ah, you've noticed my breasts,' he said calmly.

'Sorry?' I spluttered.

'My breasts,' he said, lifting his top to reveal two large breasts in a purple bra.

'Um, yes,' I mumbled.

'I used to love them, but I'm fed up with them now. Working every hour God gave to pay for them to be removed.'

'Er, have you always had them?' I asked, weirdly fascinated by them.

He put them away and told me the story. In the 1960s he had loved The Beatles, so when he reached 18 he had hitched to Hamburg to work on the Reeperbahn, as they had done. He wanted to be a singer but he hadn't managed to find a group to sing with. He took up the job of doorman at one of the red-light clubs on the strip – he had to stand outside and try to encourage passers-by to enter the dark and insalubrious den of iniquity inside. The manager of the club said that they needed an angle, something to make his club different from the others on the street. Something memorable. He offered my new friend £10,000 to have a boob job. Being 18, the guy had not really thought it through and had agreed. He used the money to start up a band but within a couple of years the money had all gone and he returned to Lancashire and obtained his HGV licence in order to pay for the reverse op. But he'd got married and had kids and never quite got round to it. He called his breasts his 'conversation starters' and I could see why. He would be in his 70s now; if you know him, please thank him for me for that lift.

But that wasn't the strangest lift I ever had. That was while I was still at college. At the end of one term I was talking to Judith Salmon, who was worried that she didn't have enough money to get home to Barnsley. By now, I loved hitching, so I offered to hitch with her across the country and then I'd go down to London. She wasn't sure at first, but that's how we ended up at the start of the East Lancs Road that March day. Winter was still hanging around and we were well wrapped up. The first lift took us to Buttonwood services on the M62. We had been waiting for only about five minutes there when an old car driven by an old man stopped to pick us up. It was to be one of my favourite lifts ever. He was going to Hull. Bingo! That would get us over to the M1 at Leeds. I put our bags in the boot and jumped in beside him, with Judith already ensconced in the back.

We chatted for a while and he thought I was very gallant for taking Judith home before heading south, especially when he found out we weren't an item. Then I made a big mistake – I asked him where he was going.

'Well,' he said, 'I'm going to Hull for a meeting. You see, I'm one of the chosen ones. Tomorrow is the "meeting". Seven of us from all over the world are meeting the envoy. I shouldn't really be telling you this, but you seem to be good people. Two years ago, we made contact. Using a special device we managed to contact the Council of the Galaxy. They are sending an envoy to meet us, in the middle of Beverley Racecourse. We have many questions to ask them. There is talk that one of the seven of us will be taken back with him to stand before the Council and put our case for membership and to be able to vote on galactic matters.'

Throughout this speech I could hear Judith suppressing laughter in the back seat. I couldn't believe my luck. If it was true, we'd know someone high up in the Galaxy Council; if it wasn't, I had about 70 miles to play with this guy.

'How do you know it's a bloke?' I asked.

'Pardon?'

'You said you'll be taken back with HIM,' I pointed out.

'No, it is definitely male.'

'OK, so where are all the delegates from Earth from?'

'Cardiff, Aberdeen, Glasgow, Bournemouth, Bristol and Gibraltar. I'm from Mold,' he said, counting them off on his fingers.

'Your map of the world is very different to mine,' I quipped.

'Ah, you are mocking me. Do you think I'm not used to it? I've heard every joke there is. But tomorrow I will meet a being from another planet.'

'On Beverley Racecourse?' Judith was now crying into her coat on the back seat. 'Why did they choose Beverley Racecourse?'

'They like it,' he said, as if I was an idiot for not understanding this.

'So they've been here before?' I asked.

'No, tomorrow is the first time. They can see it through their telescope. They can probably see this car right now.'

This went on for an hour and a half until we got to the Huddersfield turn-off. Before we got out he made us promise that we wouldn't go to the papers or tell anyone else.

As he drove away we collapsed on each other, crying with laughter.

After Steph, I went out with Julie, who was studying to be a vet at Bristol University a year below my brother Neil. So I started to hitch to Bristol instead of Ashbourne. I was living on the dole, though, and had very little money. I started to visit the sperm bank in Bristol as soon as I arrived. You weren't allowed to pleasure yourself for three days before a visit and you got paid £8 when you made a deposit. The last time I went there was Julie's birthday and I got a little carried away as I hadn't seen her for a fortnight. I missed the petri dish and some went on the carpet. I scooped it up and took out any hairs I could find, as I needed the money to take Julie out that night. I handed it in and took my money, but I never went back. For years I had a recurring nightmare that I got off a train at Bristol Temple Meads and there were all these kids who looked like me except for one standing at the back by a telephone box. He looked just like me but where his hair should have been there was carpet!

One summer's day my dad asked me to play cricket for his civil engineering firm at Regent's Park. My dad had become a civil engineer in the 1960s and his firm did a lot of work on big buildings, including hospitals, universities and football stadiums. In fact, my dad closed the Shed at Chelsea as it was too dangerous. One of my earliest memories is of him walking along the top of the Snowdon Aviary at London Zoo, without a safety rope.

The cricket game was on a pitch right by the zoo, and two elephants watched our exploits throughout. My dad kept wicket and took a couple of catches. I scored 38 runs and had a pleasant evening. After the game, we went to a pub on Baker Street and had a pint and some sandwiches and then my dad dropped me off at the start of the M4 as I was heading off to see Julie. The lifts came thick and fast and by 9.30 I had already reached Leigh Delamere services. I popped into the loos and thought about changing out of my cricket whites. No, I thought, maybe that was why I was catching lifts so quickly. I walked towards the exit onto the motorway, where there were three people waiting for lifts (sometimes at the start of the M1 at Brent Cross there could be 20 or 30 people waiting).

The etiquette in those days was to join the line furthest away from the motorway, then move up when someone caught a lift. These guys looked new to hitching, though – none of them had a sign. I always wrote a sign; I would carry a thick marker pen and find a cardboard box to tear up. I would write the destination and the word 'PLEASE' underneath. It paid to be polite. If they weren't that experienced, I thought, I can walk past to the other end. If anyone had challenged me I would have gone back to the far end, but they didn't and so I had a great position. Literally as soon as I put my thumb out I saw a car coming. As the driver passed each person I could see his moral anguish growing. He went by me, slowing down, and stopped a further 50 yards down the road, almost at the motorway. I started to run towards the car and looked back over my shoulder, checking to see if any of the other three hitch-hikers had noticed, but they were looking in the direction of the service station. But as I turned my head to the front, I found that it was in exactly the same position as a road sign. With my momentum stopped so suddenly, the bag in my hand lifted my body up in an arc, the fulcrum being my head and the sign. I crashed to the ground on my back.

For a couple of seconds I didn't know where I was. I felt my forehead; there was a large gash and blood was already pumping out. Then I remembered the lift and struggled to my feet. I stumbled to the side of the car but the guy took one look at my face, now covered in blood, and drove off. By then, the other three hitchers had come running up. They had been alerted by the almighty clang as my head met the metal road sign. I needed something to staunch the flow of blood, so I found a sock in my bag and placed it on the wound. I looked down at my cricket whites – they were more red than white now. I needed to get cleaned up and stop the blood loss, so I headed for the services.

When I walked through the door all hell broke loose. I can understand why now, but at the time I think I was in shock. I looked like a surgeon at the end of an eight-hour shift fitting stomach bands. I was covered in blood. People started asking me questions:

'Has there been a car crash?'

'Is the motorway closed?'

'Are you all right?'

I think it was the loss of blood, but at this juncture my legs went from under me. I fell to the floor. No one caught me, but then I guess I was covered in blood. Someone put a blanket round me and sat me up against the wall. I had quite a crowd. Someone else brought me a mug of hot sweet tea from the restaurant. They told me an ambulance had been called. When it arrived, the paramedic asked whether I wanted to be taken to Chippenham or Bristol A&E, as they were affiliated to both. I couldn't believe my luck – Julie lived just up the hill from the hospital, so I told them Bristol. She received a bit of a shock when I walked through the door, saying, 'Happy Halloween!' She pointed out it was July. I took the injury as a warning. Karma. I never jumped the queue again.

I love my sport. I'll watch any sport and I have seen most at their highest level. And I've tried to play most sports at some point in my life, too. At the age of 20 I played my first and last game of rugby league.

It wasn't even proper rugby league – it was sevens. The college was invited to play in a tournament in Manchester, but as Notre Dame had only 30 lads and 360 women it was hard to get a team together. We had only one student who had ever played league before, so he begged six of us who had played union to join him. So one Saturday in the summer we all piled into a minibus and drove over to Salesian College for the tournament. On the way, Dean, who had been on Halifax's books before going to college, told us the rules of rugby league. He had some plans as to how we should play, too.

It was hopeless – we lost all three of the group games by at least 10 points (we were only playing seven minutes each way) and we were out of the competition. Dean was distraught and said he couldn't stay around, as he knew some of the players from the other teams. There was a beer tent and the others were staying to watch the semis and the final, but I didn't have any money and said I'd hitch-hike back with him if he wanted. He jumped at the chance to get away. Our first lift took us to the East Lancs Road at Astley. I asked the driver to drop us at the Little Chef there, where I figured we would have more chance of catching a lift. Service stations were always my hitching point of choice: when people are comfortable and well fed they are more likely to pick up someone who's standing by the road in the cold.

But after nearly an hour Dean was moaning. Astley Little Chef is no Watford Gap! We emptied our pockets of change – we had 82p between us. We entered the cafe, sat down and perused the menu. Eggs, bacon, fried slice and baked beans were 45p, so 90p for the two of us. Then I noticed that beans on the sides menu were 8p, so I ordered two all-day breakfasts and asked them to hold the beans as we didn't want them. When they arrived, we tucked in and cleaned our plates. But when I asked for the bill it came to 90p. Dean and I argued that we hadn't had the beans, and that as they cost 8p it should have been only 37p each. The guy behind the counter was having none of it. He explained it was a set meal and therefore we had to pay full price. So Dean, being a good Yorkshireman, asked for the beans – he said that if we had to pay for them we wanted to eat them. The 'chef' went into the kitchen and brought back two portions of lukewarm baked beans. We took them back to our table and discussed what we should do. Dean was all for doing a runner, but my inner Boy Scout came through. We left the 82p on the table and then did a runner. We ran along the East Lancs Road, laughing, with the guy chasing us half-heartedly.

As we ran along, I put my thumb out and suddenly a blue Volvo stopped for us. We jumped in, the driver whizzed off and we were away.

'Robbed a bank, have we?' asked the driver. We told him the story and he laughed at our 'big crime', as he called it. Dean and I had both jumped in the back, so we couldn't see his face, but I recognised his voice. I wiggled in my seat to get a look at him in the rear-view mirror. It was Mike Harding! He had had a hit with 'Rochdale Cowboy' a couple of years before and now he had left the folk clubs for television and stand-up comedy. I was awestruck. Dean, on the other hand, didn't have a clue who he was. The two of them chatted away about rugby league while I sat there saying over and over in my head, 'It's Mike Harding! It's Mike Harding! It's Mike Harding!' He dropped us at the M6 junction and with one more lift we were within walking distance of college.

The years from 1979 to 1981 were the height of my hitching. I would think nothing of getting up at 5am and hitching to London for an event. I went down for 'The Secret Policeman's Ball', a comedy show for Amnesty International – the lifts were slow that day and I took my seat with two minutes to spare. It was a very funny show – Peter Cook playing a judge summing up the Jeremy Thorpe case, Billy Connolly celebrating being the only non-Oxbridge comic on the bill, and Rowan Atkinson doing his headmaster skit. Afterwards I went to the back of the theatre and in the mêlée managed to sneak past the stage-door manager. I met all my comedy heroes that night. Michael Palin started introducing me to everyone on the stairs – Billy, Rowan, John Cleese, Graham Chapman, Terry Jones.

In June I went to Epsom for the Derby, and later in the month I went down for Wimbledon, where I queued all night and then ran to Centre Court to see Hana Mandlíková play a quarter-final. I loved watching her play.

I also followed The Boomtown Rats around. I saw them in Liverpool, then the next night in Stoke and then at Bristol's Colston Hall. I had nearly cut the top of my right thumb off opening a can of carrots and had this big white bandage wrapped round it and I wore a tuxedo jacket that was five sizes too big for me. I suppose I wasn't hard to spot from the stage, but I was surprised when Bob Geldof reached down and dragged me onto the stage to dance with him to 'The Elephant's Graveyard' during the encore. At the end of the dance, I walked into the wings and watched them do 'Rat Trap' to close the show. Mr Geldof came off and I walked with him to his dressing room and we talked for five minutes about Kerouac and journalism. Then he left to get on the tour bus. I'd loved being in front of such a big crowd and wanted more, but I still didn't have a clue at that point how to make it happen.

3

Portsmouth

Being an island nation, each European trip involves a flight or a ferry. Back in the 1970s the ferry was the cheaper option and I'd decided to take the Portsmouth–Cherbourg route, but this meant some tricky hitch-hiking to get down from Liverpool. My first lift had taken me to Stoke and then I caught a lift in an artic as far as Northampton. The driver was headed for London but I wanted to avoid the capital, so I headed south on the A43 in a van to Oxford. From there I picked up a lift in another lorry to Southampton, and then a car to Portsmouth. The boat left at 8.30am and I reached the dockyard gates at 8.15. They told me I was too late. Damn! The next ship was at 8.30 in the evening.

I guess I had chosen Portsmouth because it's my home town. In fact, the maternity home where I was

born was just behind Sir Alec Rose's fruit and veg shop. Rose sailed round the world single-handedly in 1967–68 in a boat called *Lively Lady* and I remember my brother and me, Mum, Dad and Grandma Cobb going out to meet him as he returned triumphantly to Portsmouth. Someone we knew had commandeered the Hayling Island ferry for the day. It was a grey, windy day out in the Solent, but I understood what an achievement it was to complete such a mammoth task. It imbued in me a wish to explore the globe. (The maternity home has now been turned into a casino, which – in my case – seems wholly appropriate, but maybe not for my brother Neil, who was also born there and is now a vicar.)

I had 12 hours to kill, so I decided to walk over to see my grandmother in Fratton. The house she lived in was on Guildford Road and had once been a shop – it still had the shop windows and counters at the front, and then there was a long corridor back to the kitchen, past my grandma's bedroom. She slept on the ground floor as she had gone blind two years before I was born. She spent most of her time in the kitchen with her radio and a black and white telly that had no picture. These were only put on for the racing – Grace Smart loved racing!

One of my earliest memories is carrying my grandma's bet and seven shillings (35p nowadays) 50 yards down the road to the bookies. She always did a three-horse patent – seven bets: three singles, three doubles and a treble. I must have been about eight at the time and I was very worried about dropping the money. When I got to the small independent bookie, I pushed the door open and entered its dark recesses. I remember it being murky with poor lighting and a thick pall of cigarette smoke. I nervously walked towards the counter. One of the old men sitting on a high stool spotted me and said, 'It's Grace's lad.' I could just about reach the counter and put the bet down with the money. I had turned to walk out when they called me back for the receipt, and then I ran out the door as fast as I could and back to Grandma's house.

That afternoon, we watched the racing together. Two of the three horses won and I returned to the shop to pick up the £1 and 9 shillings. Grandma gave me the 9 shillings and kept the quid. I was hooked. I've been lucky enough to go to all the classics, to Grand Nationals and Cheltenham Festivals and to most tracks in the country. I've been to the Galway Festival and the Perth and Adelaide Gold Cups, and to tracks in Bangkok and Singapore, to Sha Tin and Happy Valley in Hong Kong, and to a Kentucky Derby in Louisville. I love racing as much as she did.

Her carers rarely had time to do their work when they called in on her, as their first job would always be to read out every horse in every race and some of the form. But it did pay off. She had an incredible memory for good horses and followed some smaller trainers assiduously. In 1974 my mum was surprised by a knock at the door. It was a man delivering a trampoline. It turned out my grandma had put a 5p trifecta on the first three past the post in the Derby. All three came in, with the winner at 50/1, and she got nearly £200 for her six shillings. So she ordered three trampolines for her grandchildren.

That June morning in 1982 she was surprised to see me. I put my rucksack down and told her I was off to Europe for an adventure. She said my dad had told her, and that he wasn't too happy about it. Then she laughed: 'We black sheep should stick together.' She chuckled. 'Let's have a drink.'

It was 9.30 in the morning – I liked her style. I fetched down the bottle of brandy from the top of the fridge and a bottle of milk from inside it. Taking two half-pint glasses from the shelf, I filled them a third full of brandy and then topped them up with milk – a kangaroo (because they look soft but have one hell of a kick). We spent the next 10 hours drinking and telling each other stories. She had had quite a life: she had run away from home at 13, with two Italian boys on scooters, to go to Blackpool. Then she had run away to London at 16 and met my granddad at Piccadilly Circus, outside Lyons' Corner House. There were 30 years between their ages: he had been born in 1881 and had fought in the Boer War, signing the pledge not to drink alcohol on joining the army for the extra fourpence a month.

He was high up in the Temperance Society on being demobbed and he never touched a drop his whole life.

When he met my grandmother he was living in Potters Bar and running a small shop. My grandmother moved in as his housekeeper, but when her father found out he caught the train to Potters Bar and forced them to get married. They then moved back to Portsmouth and bought a shop there. By the start of World War II Granddad also had a shop in Gosport. During the war he was an ARP warden and would often be up on the roofs of buildings putting out fires started by incendiary bombs. Portsmouth was bombed heavily and so he built a wonderful corrugated-iron Anderson shelter in the backyard, in which my brother and I played as kids. Sadly, he died before I was born – I would love to have met him.

My grandmother had a very different war. She was a good card player and had taught herself to deal second cards and bottom cards. She was working in the dockyards, and when the Americans joined the war their troop ships would come to Portsmouth. Apparently, some London gangsters would come down to play poker with the big brass on these ships and my gran would deal for them. We used a special Braille pack of cards so she could play with us when she came to stay. She loved gambling – we would play Newmarket for matches, and a game of rummy with two packs for 50p a game.

In the 1960s we would travel down to Portsmouth every weekend and we would spend half-terms and holidays there too. I sometimes wonder if all that time travelling in a car gave me my love for hitch-hiking.

One half-term when I was nearly five we had a disastrous drive down. My mum was driving our Ford Anglia, with my brother – who was nearly three years old – in the toddler seat strapped into the passenger seat and me in the back with my favourite blue stuffed rabbit. We had passed Petersfield and reached the road round Butser Hill where the Queen Elizabeth Country Park is now. There was a large number of articulated lorries from a circus parked on the north carriageway, narrowing the road to one and a half lanes. For some reason an impatient driver behind us decided to overtake, but as he pulled level with us he saw traffic coming on the other side of the road. He had nowhere to go, so he forced my mum off the road. We crashed through the hedge and careered down the field behind it. I was reading a story to Bunny. Suddenly the car was bucking and bouncing, and somehow the back seat collapsed, the boot opened and I flew out, landing stunned in the grass. The car continued down the field until it hit a fence at the bottom.

A lot of cars had seen what had happened and their occupants came running, along with many of the circus folk, who had been having a rest. Some of

them came to me but most went past me down to
the car. I was now crying as I had l lost Bunny. I'm
so glad they kept me away from the car – my mum,
seeing the approaching impact, had thrown herself
across my brother, but both of them had gone through
the windscreen. My mum had been lucky; by diving
to her left she had avoided the engine, which had
burst through the dashboard, knocking the steering
wheel into the seat back. Someone drove off to phone
for an ambulance.

My rabbit was found and I was carried up to one
of the circus caravans, where I was looked after by a
team of acrobats. The nearest ambulance station was
in Portsmouth and it took half an hour for one to
arrive. Then they had to get Mum and Neil out of
the car. Eventually I was taken to the ambulance,
where I was put in the front with the driver. I was
even allowed to work the siren once we reached
Portsmouth. My mum's mum arrived at the hospital
shortly after us and rang my dad's office to let him
know what had happened. She said that there had
been a serious accident. My dad was working in
Newcastle that day, but he jumped in the car and
drove all the way to Portsmouth in nine hours.
Unbelievable when you think that there weren't
any motorways in those days! The worry that he
must have suffered on that drive, not knowing what
he was going to find when he reached the hospital,
is unthinkable.

My mum and brother were in hospital for months. There was a lot of windscreen glass to remove first and then they both had corrective surgery. It is a testament to our wonderful NHS that they kept their looks with minimal scarring. I, on the other hand, was looked after by my dad and my grandma, who spoiled me rotten, and we grew very close.

I had been very lucky in this brush with death, but three years later I was not so lucky! It was my dad's birthday and he had left work early and driven back from London at lunchtime. When we arrived home from school my brother and I were told to change out of our uniforms as we were going blackberry picking. My mum had bought us new wellington boots that morning, and although it was a warm, sunny day, my brother and I begged to wear them. As it was my dad's birthday, he granted our wish.

We piled in the Ford Anglia and headed off to some army land near the Royal Aircraft Establishment (RAE). (This became Farnborough airfield, where I later worked in the car parks at the Farnborough Airshow, eventually progressing after four years to the press car park, just 100 yards from the runway. Everyone tried to get in there as it afforded brilliant views of the fly-pasts. That year Concorde was due to come in, hit the runway and immediately take off again, as the runway was too short for it to land. Consequently, in the morning I had a queue of Rollers, Daimlers and Bentleys trying it on. The bribes were amazing – a gold tiepin, a bottle of Mumm champagne, a case of beer and an embroidered flying jacket.)

We wandered into the woods looking for a good bramble patch. Armed with two carrier bags, my mum and dad began gathering blackberries. My brother and I helped for a bit but then wandered off, playing with sticks and fir cones – you know, basically fighting but not in a violent way, just being boys. Our playing led us down a path until we suddenly came across the Basingstoke Canal that cuts across the heath. We threw some stones in and looked for frogs. There was a pumping station off the towpath and opposite that on the canal bank was a metal fence. Leading down from this fence into the water was an even slope covered with paving stones at an angle of 45 degrees, which probably encased the outlet for the pump. 'Aha,' I thought. 'This would be the perfect place to test if my wellies are fully waterproof.' I told my brother my plan.

I stepped around the fence and moved to the middle. Holding onto the lowest crossbar, I began to walk backwards down the slope into the water, going far enough for the water to nearly reach the top of the boots. They didn't let in a drop. What I hadn't realised was that under the water the paving stones were covered in a slime that was extremely slippery. When I tried to climb back up I lost my footing and found myself under the water among the floating weeds. I didn't know how to swim, but I pulled myself to the surface. The look on my brother's face was a picture; I could see he was working out how much trouble we were already in.

'Get Dad!' I shouted, slipping back under the murky water. My mouth was open and I took in a massive swallow of the bitter liquid. The wellingtons made kicking impossible, so I was using my arms a lot. Full-on panic hit me, and I made a huge effort to get up. I barely broke the surface and gasped for air. As I went down for the third time my whole life flashed before my eyes, but, being only seven, there wasn't much to see – ice creams, beaches, riding my bike for the first time and Helen Legget's knickers. I sank slowly to the bottom. When I couldn't hold my breath anymore I actually relaxed. I could feel my lungs filling up with water, and then everything went black. There was no light in the distance, no family members beckoning me towards them, no angels standing round a gate. Nothing. An empty, silent blackness.

My brother, meanwhile, was haring off up the path as fast as his skinny little five-year-old legs could carry him. He found my parents and through tears told them what had happened. My dad grabbed him and ran down the path, my mum in tow. When they arrived at the canal there was no sign of me. My dad started to strip off. They saw some bubbles, probably air escaping from those darn wellies, and my dad dived in. After searching the bottom for a minute, fighting the reeds around him, he found my limp body. He swam to the surface and passed me up to my mum. She checked my pulse. There wasn't one.

I've always considered myself lucky, and this is one of those moments that prove it. I know that sounds crazy. I mean, there I was, lying dead on the towpath of a canal named after Basingstoke! But two coincidences saved my life that day: first, my dad had worked for the British Telephone Company in his 20s, mainly because they wanted him in their football team. As part of his training he'd learned deep-sea diving, so that he could spend a day checking the Portsmouth to Isle of Wight phone cable. He threw me onto my front and started to pump the water out of my lungs. The second coincidence was that the night before my mum had been to see *Dr. No* at the pictures and had seen Ursula Andress administer the kiss of life to Sean Connery. She did what she had seen on the silver screen and then my dad began thumping on my chest to get my heart beating. After another minute of frantic activity I spluttered back to life and then immediately passed out. But at least they had a pulse. My father gathered me up in his arms, headed back to the car and drove like a maniac to the military hospital in Aldershot. Halfway there I woke up and threw up the contents of my stomach, some foul-smelling muddy water. My mum was wearing her best summer frock as she and Dad had planned to go out for a birthday meal later. I had ruined it with my vomit but she seemed very relieved and hugged me tight, keeping me talking all the way to the hospital.

I was kept in for a week. Each day I was wheeled into a room and the liquid and detritus from the canal was pumped out of my lungs. After five days my dad came and picked me up from the hospital and drove me to the army swimming baths, a Victorian building with a balcony around a 25-metre pool. We got changed and he took me to the deep end; he held my hand and we jumped in. Within an hour he had taught me how to swim. I'm so glad that he did; if he'd left it I think I might have become afraid of water. I still get the odd flashback if I'm in the sea or a pool and someone splashes me – I get a rush of adrenaline and I feel really uncomfortable – but I went on to swim for the Scouts and the school. I learned to sail, canoe and surf – all things I love to this day. So I'm grateful that he did it.

I guess this is why I'm not religious; when I died – and the doctors said I'd probably been dead for about three minutes – there was nothing. Later I read Jack Kerouac's *The Dharma Bums* and he says, 'Are we fallen angels who didn't want to believe that nothing is nothing and so were born to lose our loved ones and dear friends one by one and finally our own life, to see it proved?' That's how I see it. If ever the topic of an afterlife is mooted, I'll always say no. The incident probably made me fearless in dangerous situations, too.

I thought, 'Well, I've already been dead and survived that, so what's the worst that can happen?'

I loved those weekends in Portsmouth. My parents were both very sporty and we did lots of activities, especially in the summer. We would head to the beach, we would swim, play football and cricket, or we would go on the boating lake by the pier. My brother and I would go roller skating on the Ladies' Mile at Southsea every Saturday morning. We were very good at it, so when I was 16 and they asked in the local paper for under-18s who could roller skate, I applied. The occasion was the opening of Farnborough recreation centre, a complex that had been built behind Queensmead with a swimming pool and a large gymnasium. For the grand opening they were going to showcase the different sports available with international matches, and as roller skating was to be one of the sports they needed players for a roller-hockey tournament.

Seven of us turned up at the centre the week before it opened, but it was clear that I was the only one who could skate both forwards and backwards. We were given sticks, the rules were explained to us and they told us to turn up on the Saturday at 1.30pm. When we arrived, we found out we were playing against the Dutch under-18 national team and the Belgian under-18 national team. This was our first ever game! We lost to Holland 21–0 and to Belgium 23–1, playing only 15 minutes each way.

After the first five goals I just enjoyed the occasion. There was a crowd of about 200 there, mainly to see the new centre, but they had a right old laugh at our antics.

I did have my moment playing roller hockey later on, but that came with great pain. The school had organised a sports weekend at Calshot Spit. The two large hangars that had been used during World War II for flying boats had been turned into an indoor cycling track, a climbing wall and an archery and rifle range. They also had canoes and sail boats. The Nissen huts that had been used by the aircrews and the mechanics were now converted into dormitories. We arrived on the Friday night. I was 17 and really excited about the coming events. Saturday morning was spent canoeing out on the Solent, and then in the afternoon was the cycling. In order to fit the track into the hangar, the bends at each end were very steep – 63 degrees, if I remember right. The track had a sandpaper-like finish, so the rubber tyres gripped and didn't slide down. We were racing around the track at top speed and I decided to go high and then cut down as I came off the bend, using gravity to raise my speed. As I cut down, someone came underneath me and caught my wheel. As I fell I put my arms out, but as soon as they hit the track they caught on the rough surface and I rolled over them. I was winded and my left wrist was screaming – the technical-drawing teacher who was in charge said I'd probably sprained it, so he put some magic spray on it and told me to run it under the cold tap.

That evening there was a roller-hockey tournament in the centre of the cycle track. I was in agony but I had to play as I was the only one who could skate. My wrist was getting sprayed every five minutes throughout the tournament but we won our first two matches and then the final – the score was 5–1 and I got a hat-trick. We celebrated with hot chocolate in the cafeteria and then I was sent to bed with two aspirins. I awoke the next morning in even greater pain. We had to fold up our bedding as we were leaving that afternoon, but I couldn't do it. I tried and I cried. I went to see the teacher, got my wrist sprayed and then was told to go off for my next activity – rifle shooting. Unfortunately, they were air rifles that had to be cocked each time before you could fire them. I think I managed three shots while the others fired off a hundred. Then it was the rock-climbing wall. We had safety ropes – a good job too, as I reached halfway up the wall and then realised that the only way I could go up or down was to put weight on my damaged hand. I tried and passed out. They lowered me to the ground and I was told to go and wait in the coach. The journey home was completed in intense pain. I walked home and told my mum and dad.

'What did the teacher say?' asked my dad.

'He said it was sprained. But I think it's broken,' I muttered.

'Well, see how it is in the morning.'

It was agony in the morning. I somehow got dressed and left with everyone else to go to school, but when I reached the school gates I just carried on walking all the way to Frimley Park hospital. They X-rayed my wrist and told me I had broken a bone. I told them how it happened. 'Ah,' said the doctor. 'That might be why it's a jagged break. I think that you fractured it badly and then you've opened up the fracture, causing a break.' I was in plaster for the next three months.

It was only a few months later that I ended up back in Frimley Park hospital. My dad was organising a Scouts cross-country event and needed marshals around the course to tick off runners as they passed. I was dating Jackie, my first girlfriend, at the time. I asked if she could come with me and Dad said, 'Yes, as long as you concentrate on what you are doing.' So the two of us cycled up the Fleet Road and then cut into the army land to the west. After half a mile we found the bridge from the map reference my father had given me. We were early. The bridge was over a small stream, eight feet across; it wasn't deep but the banks were steep. In showing off to my girlfriend, I decided to jump the stream. I took a big run-up and launched myself across the gap. I just made it. In order not to fall back into the stream, I threw myself forward on landing. There was a small oak sapling, maybe four feet high, and as I fell I was aware of a twig brushing my face.

I stood up triumphantly, punching the air, but Jackie just look shocked. She walked slowly towards me, pointing at my face. I became aware that the world was slowly turning pink. The twig had gone across my face and over my eye and it had cut the cornea. There are a lot of capillaries in the eyeball and these were now leaking profusely. It also began to sting as I blinked the blood away.

'You'll have to go to the hospital,' she said, looking very serious.

'But I can't see to ride,' I replied.

'Hitch a lift up on the road' was her advice.

So I gave her the list of runners and the pen and headed off to the road half a mile away. By the time I reached the road I was desperate and the pain was getting worse. I stood on the side of the road and waved both arms, trying to get someone to stop. Unfortunately, the film *The Omen* had been released the month before and in it there is a scene were someone tries to flag down cars on a deserted road after having their eyes plucked out by crows. To oncoming drivers it must have looked like I was recreating that moment as I stood there covered in blood. Eventually I stopped someone and begged them to take me to Frimley Park. At the hospital they cleaned up my eye and gave me some drops and I had to wear an eyepatch for a month.

They say that the average person spends 27 days in hospital in the course of a lifetime – I think I had passed that by the time I was 20.

I spent the whole of that day I missed the ferry with my grandmother in Portsmouth. She told wonderful stories about love and craziness. We laughed and cried and laughed some more. She urged me to make the most of the adventure I was undertaking and told me to stay away as long as I could, and then come back and tell her all about it.

I weaved my way back to the ferry terminal and, once onboard, drunkenly collapsed onto a lounger surrounded by giddily happy schoolchildren on their first trips abroad.

4

The Ferry

As we pulled out of Portsmouth, past the castle where the *Mary Rose* sank, my thoughts turned to previous sorties into Europe. I had been six times in my 22 years: twice on family holidays to Brittany, once for a school ski trip to the French Alps, a weekend with the Scouts in Delft in Holland, and twice on Interrail.

The first time I went Interrailing was with Chris Heald and Stephanie Lunt. Chris was an old friend from Farnborough and Stephanie, who was at college with me, and her friend were going to join us for safety, but then her friend pulled out and so the three of us set off in August 1979. We would go to a city, spend the day sightseeing, then pick somewhere eight hours away and board the train around midnight; that meant we could sleep on the train and didn't have to pay for hotels. We would get off at 8am in the next city and repeat. I did the whole month living on £3 a day. We went as far north as Elsinore in Denmark, east to Athens, west to Madrid and south to Fez – 13,000 miles and 10 countries. It was a great trip. Chris and I agreed beforehand that this was an exploratory trip to find places we wanted to go back to.

I loved Munich, Luxembourg City, Monaco, Heidelberg castle and Venice, but the big eye-opener was Morocco. A real culture shock and like nowhere I'd ever been before. We arrived in Tangier in the evening but there were no trains leaving that night, so we decided to stay in a hostel – all three of us in the same room. We toured the casbah, greeted everywhere by shouts of 'Bobby Charlton' and 'fish and chips'. Steph had shoulder-length fair hair and a pale complexion and the locals couldn't stop staring – some even tried to touch her hair. Chris and I had our work cut out as bodyguards and we returned to the hostel exhausted. In the morning, Steph went for a shower and then I heard her screaming. I ran down the hall to find the owner leaving the bathroom rapidly. He had been trying to get into the shower with her. I stood guard until she had finished and then the three of us packed up and left. We walked to the station and caught a train to Casablanca.

The ticket office explained that our Interrail tickets were valid but only in third class. A train came in and we asked where third class was; it turned out that there were only first- and second-class carriages. The third class would be along in a minute. Half an hour later a tired-looking steam engine pulled into the platform, followed by five cattle trucks. Some ingenious person had cut window shapes in the wooden sides of the trucks and a hole for a door, but there was no actual door. We bundled inside with the other passengers to be confronted with six cast-iron park benches screwed to the floor. We managed to get one for ourselves. The air temperature must have been in the high 30s and was unbearable, though it wasn't that bad once we started moving, especially when the tracks followed the coast just north of the capital, Rabat.

Casablanca was one of the biggest disappointments of my life. I love the film so much, which is why I had wanted to go there, but when we arrived it seemed to be just a vast oil refinery with a dirty town stuck on the side. Wherever you went you could see the giant tanks of oil. The casbah was tiny and dirty and there was nothing to see. I'm sure it's all changed now, but I just remember being so low. We decided to go to Fez: there was a train leaving at 8pm that stopped at 1am in Mechra Bel Ksiri on the edge of the Sahara, and we'd then have a wait of four and a half hours to pick up a train to Fez.

When we arrived in Mechra Bel Ksiri, however, we found that quite a few Moroccans had had the same idea. There was a waiting room, but it was for first-class passengers only. After 10 minutes I had to point out that Steph was attracting a lot of unwanted attention and pleaded with the station master to let us use it. Once inside we were left alone. There were a Dutch couple and an American guy already in there. I told the other two to get some sleep; I would sit up and keep watch over our bags and then sleep on the next train. I began reading my book while everyone else fell asleep on the cool marble floor tiles. It was a good job I stayed awake, as after an hour or so I saw some rapid movement out of the corner of my eye. Something was scuttling across the floor towards my sleeping friends – it was the biggest scorpion I have ever seen. I shouted, 'Wake up!' and leapt off the bench and kicked it against the wall. Strangely, no one slept after that.

Fez is a fantastic place built on the edge of the Sahara. It was stunning. We left our bags at the station and ventured out into the casbah, with Steph now covered head to toe, as we had realised that it was her bare skin and our lack of understanding of Islam that were causing the problem. We employed a young boy of about eight who spoke very good English as a guide. He gave us a wonderful tour of the narrow streets of the market and we ended up on a high terrace by the fort, drinking mint tea and eating little cakes. From our viewpoint we could see the Atlas mountains to the northeast and the vast expanse of sand to the southeast. Then on the horizon we saw some black clouds starting to form. 'Sandstorm,' said our young guide. We decided to return to the station to get the train back to Tangier, so we said goodbye to our little friend and headed back through the casbah.

As we walked down the main drag to the station (which was about as wide as your average pavement), we put our heads down and strode purposefully. Everyone wanted us to enter their shops and as we approached the end of the street someone grabbed Steph by the arm, quite forcefully. Chris and I grabbed her other arm and pulled her free, but this didn't go down too well. Other shopkeepers started to join in and very quickly we were facing down about 10 men, all of them angry. I told Chris to take Steph to the taxi rank that was by a roundabout 50 feet away. I stood my ground and smiled at the angry mob. There was a lot of shouting. I said I'd give them money for the disruption we had caused, to buy time for the others to get away, and then I started going through my pockets slowly, checking for money.

We had left our passports and most of our money in our bags at the station. My paper money was tucked down my socks, but I had a load of change in my pockets. The crowd was shouting at me to hurry up, but when they saw the small amount I was offering the shouts grew louder. I saw that my fellow travellers were in the taxi with the door open, so I threw the money in the chest of the man who had started the whole incident and ran for the cab. As the coins hit the ground, children came running from everywhere, tripping up the men who were trying to chase me. I jumped in the taxi and the wheels were spinning before I had closed the door.

We caught the train just as the sandstorm hit. As we pulled out into the open countryside we quickly realised that windows with glass are much better – in our third-class carriage there were just holes. Sand was whipping through these gaps at great speed, so we huddled on the floor. There was conscription in Morocco at the time and the rest of the travellers in the truck were in military uniform, either going on leave or returning to camp. Some of them had been smoking dope quite openly in front of us once the train had started moving, and these young lads started sticking their heads out of the window. When they came back in it looked like someone had sandpapered their face. They found this hilarious.

I wasn't feeling too chipper; in fact, my stomach was in a tight knot. We had avoided ice cubes in our drinks and unwashed salads, but I had eaten a kebab in Fez that the other two had eschewed. The meat had been left out on the counter and had obviously been infected by some of the many flies that were so populous in Morocco. I didn't realise how bad it was going to get, though.

We eventually outran the storm and reached Tangier at 8am. We walked from the station to the port to catch the boat back to Spain that was leaving

at 9.30. We showed our Interrail tickets at the barrier
and moved on to customs, where one of the customs
officers took an instant dislike to me – probably
because I was smiling at him. Mistake number one. By
this point I just wanted to get out of Morocco. The
hassle that Steph had undergone, the disappointment
of Casablanca, the scorpion and the casbah attack
had turned me against the country. I'm sure that it
has changed a lot in 40 years and I'd love to go back
– I really want to ski in the Atlas mountains – but
the thought of leaving that morning had made me
smile. This had obviously been seen as a provocation
and the customs officer asked to see what was in my
rucksack. I emptied out my dirty clothes (we were
three weeks into the journey by now), my sleeping
bag and a couple of books. He opened the sleeping
bag and checked it for hidden contraband and then he
made me put it all back.

Once I was repacked I thought that was it and I
started to walk towards the gate. I needed the loo
and reasoned that there would be one on the boat.
Mistake number two. He called me back gruffly. He
told Steph and Chris that they were OK to go but he
needed to see my passport. Chris knew I was weak
and offered to take my bag onto the boat while I was
led in the opposite direction to a shed on the quayside.
I was pushed through the open door into a hot little
room dominated by a large desk behind which sat a
large, tousle-haired man in a dirty white vest. He was

picking the breakfast out of his teeth with a match. The officer who had brought me in threw my passport onto the desk. The boss picked it up slowly, staring at me as he did so. He flicked through it with a look of disgust on his face. He checked my photo, looking from the passport to my face to the passport and then back to me.

Then he said, 'Your hair.'

'Yes,' I replied.

'He is dirty.'

'Sorry.'

He pointed at a door to his left. 'You go wash it.'

'Sorry?'

'You go wash it.'

So I walked into the room, where there was a toilet and a wash basin. The sink was about the size of a CD. I filled it with water and soaked my shoulder-length hair, careful not to make too much of a mess. There was no towel, so I lifted the front of my T-shirt and dried it as well as I could. My next problem was that I had no comb. I ran my fingers through my damp hair, sweeping it back off my forehead. Then I returned to the office. The customs guy looked me up and down.

'Now your shirt is dirty. You must put on a clean shirt. What would people think in Spain if I let you get on the ship? They would think, "Morocco must be a dirty place." I cannot allow it.'

'But my bag is on the boat with my friends.'

'Well, you better go and see them, and ask for a clean one.'

I ran out of his office and down the quayside towards the ship. It was five minutes before it was due to leave. Luckily, Chris and Steph had headed to the bow rail from where they could see the customs shed. They saw me coming and shouted for me to hurry up.

'I NEED A CLEAN SHIRT FROM MY BAG!' I shouted up to them.

'WHAT?' cried Steph.

Chris was already searching through my rucksack. 'THERE AREN'T ANY!'

'WHAT ABOUT THE GREEN JUMPER? THAT'S CLEAN.'

By now quite a crowd had gathered, both on the ship and on the dock. Chris rolled the green jumper into a tight ball and threw it as hard as he could. There was a big cheer as I caught it, reaching out over the water without falling in. The crew were getting ready to take down the gangplank, so I ran back down the quayside. It was 35°C, but I put the bright green pullover on instead of my shirt on entering the office.

'That's better,' my friend said, smiling like a Bond villain.

'Can I have my passport back now, please?' I asked, trying desperately to stay calm in the face of his provocation. I knew that if I lost it I'd be staying in Tangier for a while.

He pushed it across the desk, but when I reached for it he pulled it back.

'Excuse me, sir, but I'm going to miss my boat.'

He laughed and offered up my passport. I took hold of it, but he didn't let go. We were both leaning across his expansive desk and I could smell cigarettes and garlic on his breath. He looked me in the eye and very slowly said, 'I think you have never seen the eyes of a snake?'

'What?'

He released his grip on my passport and I ran out of the office and along the dockside, shouting at the crew to put the gangplank back. All the other Interrailers at the rail cheered as I ran up it and onto the ship. I made my way up on deck and found Steph and Chris. The boat began to move straight away, and as we left port I stood at the point of the bow and flicked a V-sign animatedly at the customs shack. I've never been so happy to leave a country!

That evening we caught a train from Algeciras to Madrid. By now my tummy was really rumbling and I couldn't leave the loo for more than 15 minutes at a time. I had a temperature and was sweating profusely. We arrived early in Madrid and Chris had worked out a whole list of things he wanted to see. We needed two maps for this: one for Steph and Chris and one for me. I made the tourist information people mark all the public toilets on mine, and Chris and Steph would go on ahead while I waited in a loo. Then I'd run to the tourist location, get a photo of me in front of it and sprint to the next toilet. After the Royal Palace I was getting fed up with this plan – I really wanted to see the Old Town. So I borrowed a tampon from Steph, shoved it where the sun don't shine and managed to last a couple of hours.

We finished the trip with Paris and Amsterdam – two beautiful, lively cities. I had recovered enough to enjoy them and I have many happy memories of this trip, but probably the best moment was going into the casino at Monte Carlo. The minimum bet at the roulette table was £2.50 in francs, and I was living on £3 a day. I put my chip on black and it came up. I picked up the two chips and cashed them in – I'd doubled my money, so I can say that I went to the Monte Carlo casino and walked out a winner. I bought a bottle of wine for 35p with my winnings.

👍

I loved the trip so much that the following summer I decided to do it again. I asked my oldest friend, Pete Carey, if he'd like to go and he jumped at the chance. We met at Farnborough station at 11.30 one night in late July. The ticket started at midnight, so we were going to catch the last train up to London at 12.05 and then walk to Victoria and get the boat train at 2.30am to Dover. However, when we arrived in London we found that Pete had left his sleeping bag on the bench at Farnborough. He wanted to go back but I said we should push on. I won. This was a portent of what was to come throughout the trip – somehow Pete managed to lose most of his stuff, returning at the end of the month with an empty bag.

In order to wash we would visit swimming pools and then use the showers to have a good clean-up after our swim. In Munich we visited the Olympic pool that had been used in the 1972 games. It was an amazing circular building all made of glass. After a swim and a shower we were getting dressed in the cubicles when I heard Pete shouting. Someone had reached under the door and stolen his training shoes! Once we were dressed, we told the attendant in broken German what had happened, but he said he couldn't do anything about it. We explained that these were the only shoes Pete had and we were Interrailing round Europe. He disappeared for a couple of minutes and returned with a pair of Scholl sandals. Poor Pete spent the next three weeks walking round the great cities of Europe in a pair of sandals. They must have hurt his feet as we were covering up to 12 miles a day, but he never complained.

After Munich we headed to Athens. On the timetable we had it said that the train left at 11.45 and arrived at 10.25. We bought some sandwiches and some lemonade and boarded the train. It was 1930s rolling stock and every carriage was full – I didn't mind too much as there was a luggage rack in the corridor about nine inches wide and Pete and I slept on this. There were two Scousers sleeping on the floor of the corridor below us who had a tape recorder with them, but only one tape: *Lodger* by David Bowie. They played it at full blast again and again; everyone was complaining, but they were big lads and just ignored us all. After three hours the tape began to slide and we realised with glee that the batteries were running down, but they just reached into their bag and pulled out more. To this day, I still know every lyric of every song on that album.

Overnight we travelled down through Austria and into Yugoslavia, reaching Zagreb by lunchtime the next day. As the train moved slowly through this communist country and we looked at the countryside with its crumbling houses and ox-drawn carts on the roads, it felt like we had gone back in time a couple of hundred years. We talked to a Yugoslavian businessman who told us proudly that there was no unemployment in the country – 'Not like your 3 million in Britain,' he said. We saw evidence of this when the train slowed even further as we passed some track repairs. They were putting new rails down, but not with a crane – they were being lifted into place manually by 60 workers.

'We're never going to get to Athens tonight,' I said. The other Interrailers in the compartment next to us laughed. We weren't supposed to get to Athens that night, they told us — it was a 48-hour journey from Munich to Athens. We should have noticed this on the timetable! We had run out of food, so when we reached Sofia I jumped off the train and ran up and down the platform trying to find something to eat. There was a young lad selling cold hamburgers. We had no local currency, but I waved a pound note at him and eventually he relented. I grabbed four bottles of water from another vendor and parted with another pound, then ran back onto the train as it started moving. We lived on this for the next 24 hours.

Athens was hot. We changed some money and headed to the Plaka and had a big meal, then we found a nearby hostel. It was a pound to sleep in a room or 50p to sleep on the roof; we chose the roof. I'd bought a half bottle of ouzo and we drank it all before falling asleep to the sounds of the city. On waking, we had an amazing view of the Parthenon above us on the Acropolis. As I had already been to Athens the year before, I told Pete to go sightseeing while I went to the station and sorted out our tickets to Piraeus and for the ferry to Corfu. The train was at 1pm, so Pete had about three hours to see the Parthenon and the Olympic stadium and get back to the station. I took our two bags and headed off.

It took ages to sort it all out and I was relieved that I'd gone so early. The train pulled in and I stood on the platform waiting for Pete, but there was no sign

of him. The guard blew his whistle and I suddenly
spotted my mate dashing through the crowd; I waved
and boarded the train. He appeared running alongside
the door and I leaned out and pulled him up onto
the train. There were only two seats at opposite ends
of the carriage, so we sat down in them. I was next to
a Greek widow, dressed all in black, tiny and round.
Opposite me on the facing bench was a young mother
with a baby in a basket at her feet, and next to her a
nun in a grey habit and a big wimple. I looked down
the train and saw Pete sitting there, sweating profusely.
He hadn't had a chance to grab any food or drink,
but I had. I held up a two-litre bottle of lemonade
and a giant bag of cheese puffs. His face lit up. Pete
made his way down the aisle, bumping into most of
the seats – the train was climbing the twisty track
towards the point where it crosses the Corinth Canal.
He immediately took the screw top off the bottle and
started gulping down the cold liquid.

'Take it back to your seat,' I said, proffering the giant
bag of puffs.

He tucked the bottle in the crook of his left arm
and reached for the cheese puffs. In doing so, he
managed to drop the top of the lemonade bottle, but
he took the bag anyway. Then, without thinking, he
leaned down to pick up the top. The lemonade from
the open bottle began to pour onto the baby in the
basket. Pete saw this and stood up suddenly, sending
an arc of liquid over the now screaming mother, the

nun and the widow. Brilliantly, not one drop hit me! He left sheepishly and went back to his seat, leaving me with an hour's journey under frosty stares. It still makes me laugh today. You'd never be able to replicate it in a comedy sketch – everything just happened with perfect timing.

Corfu was stunning – so stunning that Pete forgot to put any suncream on. By the evening he was the proverbial lobster! At dusk we climbed down a hill through a watermelon farm to a small beach, about 15 feet wide. We liberated one of the watermelons and ate it washed down with a bottle of retsina. As Pete was suffering from sunburn, I gave him my sleeping bag and I took our two towels and slept between them on the beach, but at about 1am the sand fleas found us. It was agony. We eventually gave up sleeping on the sand and walked back up to the roadside wall, where we slept on a rock. We woke up at dawn to a view of the Albanian coast two miles away, and then we headed back to Corfu town to take the ferry to Rimini.

We covered 11,000 miles and saw 12 countries on that trip (including Liechtenstein). If you are under 26 and you can get the money together, then I would advise you to go Interrailing at least once. It's a great way to see the continent of Europe in all its glory, its history and its sunspots. I reckon you could do it on about £15 a day. You'll meet lots of people, too, and learn about their countries, their lives and their dreams. I think I probably learned more useful things in those two Interrail trips than I did in three years at college.

The ferry was coming into Cherbourg just before midnight and the schoolchildren were being rounded up to return to their coaches. I had expected to arrive at lunchtime, when it would have been much easier to catch a lift. Midnight was a different proposition. I would need to be lucky with my first lift on continental soil. Happily, I was.

5

Saint-Lô

The ferry docked just after midnight. It was a warm night and I rushed down the gangplank, straight through customs and out of the building in an attempt to catch the vehicles leaving the boat. I had made a sign: 'PARIS S'IL VOUS PLAÎT!'

The lorries tore past me, ignoring it, so I started walking along the road with my thumb out. Nothing. Just as I reached the town a 2CV stopped. It was driven by a very nervous-looking, young French guy with glasses. I put my red rucksack on the back seat and climbed in the passenger seat. He explained in very good English that he was not heading to Paris but to Saint-Lô. He said he had been the last off the boat as his engine hadn't started at first and told me that there would be no more traffic after him – that was why he had stopped for me.

I thanked him and told him about my 'always say yes' philosophy. He had been to Salisbury to see his girlfriend who was teaching French at a school there; he was taking a course in English so he could join her. We got along very well. I told him of my childhood holidays in Brittany, and how much I liked the prehistoric stones at Carnac. He pointed out the church steeple on which the American parachutist was caught in World War II – it's in the film *The Longest Day*.

It was now about 1.30am and we weren't seeing many cars on the road, so my driver asked very nervously if I'd like to stay at his flat. I declined at first, sensing his trepidation, but the further we travelled the fewer cars we saw. When we reached his home town of Saint-Lô he asked me again, and this time I said yes. We parked up and climbed the stairs to his little flat in a newish building on the edge of town. He made us a plate of snacks and brought me a beer. I thanked him profusely.

I slept on the couch. He woke me at 8am with a coffee. I thanked him again, then walked to the N84 to hitch directly south. I had a friend, Karen, who was living with a French family in a townhouse just off the main square in Laval, and I decided to go and see her. When I was resitting my final year at college, I had shared a house with Karen, Rachel and Christine. Because I was two years older than them, they had called me Dad. Karen had studied French at university, and during her exchange year she met and fell in love with a young French lad. Earlier that year I had attended their wedding in Bolton as her second 'dad'. The groom was a member of a brass band and they had all come over from France for the ceremony and to play at the reception. It was a very jolly affair. I spent the day charged with looking after Karen's little brother who was six, even playing football with him in the church hall car park. He grew up to be Guy Garvey of Elbow. Lovely bloke.

It took two lifts to reach Laval and I joined Karen and her new adopted family for a three-hour lunch. I love French food and this was a feast – cold meats, cheeses, fresh bread warm from the *boulangerie*, and *beaucoup de vin*. I told them of my Good Samaritan the night before and they were very proud of their countryman.

I have always been lucky with the people I meet on the road.

The first time I did the Edinburgh Fringe Festival was in 1980. I hitched up to Edinburgh with a tent and camped at the campsite near the artificial ski slope to the south of the city. It was quite a way out, but I woke up early and caught a bus into town. I had never been to Edinburgh before and was immediately taken

by its dramatic beauty. I spent the day wandering round the Royal Mile and the Mound, watching the street shows and listening to those handing out flyers. I didn't have much money, having just returned from Interrailing, so I tried to find free shows. The Fringe club had a late-night bar where if you performed you got in free, so I went along. The room was in the Edinburgh University Student Union – it was loud and it smelled of drunks. I've never been so scared in my life. I was on third after an amateur theatre company that did scenes from its production of *A Midsummer Night's Dream*, which did not go down well.

I went out onto the stage and took the mike from its stand. I coughed nervously. This seemed to be a sign for the heckling to start. I started telling a joke I'd heard on the TV show *The Comedians*. When I got to the end, three people laughed and the other 80 upped their game. I could hardly hear myself think. I told my second joke, about a tortoise being mugged by snails. When the police arrive and say, 'Can you describe your assailants?', the tortoise says, 'I don't think so, it all happened so fast.' But by now no one was listening.

I climbed the stairs back to the dressing room. Nobody made eye contact and I felt ashamed and guilty – guilty that I hadn't entertained anyone. I decided that I would never be a stand-up; I'd have to find another way to become an entertainer, but I was hooked. I loved the feeling of the Fringe. Anyone can take a show up to Edinburgh and perform at the Festival – by 2019 I'd reached my 40th consecutive Fringe. I love it. I've done street shows, performing as a juggler and with Angelo Abela in The Vicious Boys; I've acted in *Twelve Angry Men* and *The Dumb Waiter*; and I've played at the Assembly Rooms, the Gilded Balloon and the Pleasance, as well as lots of other venues. I absolutely love it. I have now spent over two years of my life at Edinburgh Fringe Festivals if you add up all the days.

But that night in my tent was horrible. I was inconsolable. I tossed and turned in my sleeping bag as a light rain began to fall, pattering gently on the side of the tent. I felt wretched and very alone, and I don't think I told another joke to anyone for nearly six months. I had made the classic error of not looking confident – an audience can smell fear and will feed on that fear if they are drunk. Any comic will tell you that there is nothing worse than dying on stage; sometimes it takes two or three days to get over it. Eventually I fell asleep.

The next day I packed up my stuff, left it in the left-luggage office at Waverley Station, and then spent the day exploring the city. I found Rose Street, full of shops, bars and restaurants; I went to the Grassmarket and had a look in the Traverse Theatre. There were people in costume everywhere advertising their shows. At about eight in the evening, I fetched my bag from the station and caught a bus to the start of the A68 to begin hitching back to Liverpool.

I'd been there for about two hours when two young lads who were going to Selkirk stopped for me. They had been to Edinburgh to see some shows and to hear a band made up of their friends. The elder boy was Billy, who was 18, and his brother (whose name I can't remember) was 13. They had obviously had a great day and I was lifted out of my dark mood by their laughing and chattering. They told me that I wouldn't get a lift in Selkirk until the morning as the road wasn't that busy, and they asked if I'd like to spend the night at their parents' house. I wasn't sure but they said they lived in a big house with its own stretch of salmon river. They had me. This sounded too good to be true but I was now curious. After an hour's drive we reached Selkirk and stopped at a house on the edge of town. It was only two storeys high but very long.

We entered through the kitchen door. There was no sign of their parents.

'They've gone to bed,' said Billy. 'I'll leave them a note.'

He grabbed me a glass of water from the sink and then took me to my room, which was huge. There was a massive double bed with lots of eiderdowns on it, and around the walls were animal skins – a zebra, a leopard and an eland. There were some African masks and a few spears and shields. 'This is the Africa room,' commented Billy, with a big grin. 'Breakfast will be around 8.30. See you then.'

I switched on the bedside light, climbed into bed and read my book, eventually falling asleep at about two. I couldn't believe the difference between the two nights' sleep: one tossing and turning in a damp tent; the next staying in opulent luxury.

I slept well but woke to hear someone going past my door along the creaky oak floorboards. I didn't have a watch and we didn't have mobile phones in those days, so there was no knowing what time it was. I pulled back the curtains; it was light, a beautiful sunny day. I was looking at a long green field falling away to a bend in a river with a small wood on the other side. It took my breath away, but then I started to panic. I had been brought up properly and knew it would be rude to stay in bed after breakfast had been served. But had I already missed it? I didn't know. I pulled my jeans on and opened the door a crack. There was no one there. I darted across to the bathroom and washed and made myself look respectable. Then I zipped back to my room, dressed, packed my rucksack and headed downstairs.

As I entered the kitchen I could see a small man in a dressing gown standing at an Aga cooking some bacon. He had his back to me and jumped as I put my rucksack down and it immediately fell over with a crash. To my amazement, when he turned round I realised he was (Lord) David Steel, leader of the Liberal Party.

'You must be the hitch-hiker,' he said casually. 'Billy left me a note. Now what do you want for breakfast? There's eggs, bacon, mushrooms, tomatoes, or porridge if you'd prefer.'

'Um, the fry-up sounds good,' I muttered, still trying to work out what was going on.

Then he cooked me my food and we sat and ate together, discussing Parliament and his party's chances at the next election. It was so surreal. He told me the African trophies in my room had been a gift for sorting out a trade deal. We talked about travelling, unemployment and Thatcher until the other members of the family began to arrive. His wife was lovely, fussing over me to eat more and asking me about hitch-hiking. Billy and his younger brother and sister arrived, and after breakfast we all went down to the river to see if we could see any salmon running. When we returned to the house to get my bag, Lady Steel had made me some sandwiches. What a marvellous family. I went up to the A7 and headed back to Liverpool.

👍

The second time I went to America I was treated with real kindness by Paul Iaffaldano.

In the first term of my second year at college, my mum sent me £150 from her mother's will. Nellie

Cobb was a wonderful woman. She had met my grandfather while in service in Cosham near Portsmouth. He had spent his life at sea until after World War II, when he trained Royal Navy sailors to fire guns on the range in Portsmouth. He died when I was six, but I do remember sitting on his knee, and he told me that if I could I should definitely visit Hong Kong, Shanghai and Rio de Janeiro. When I completed the trio in Rio, I raised a beer to him (he's right, of course – if you can, visit all three).

Nellie had worked as a cleaner and brought up my mum practically by herself; then she worked at Metal Box for 20 years. She was a very cheerful woman who loved a Player's No. 6 cigarette, and although she overboiled all her vegetables, she made the best rice pudding I've ever tasted. We would have it cold with golden syrup.

When her money arrived I decided that rather than stick it in the bank and gradually use it up, I should do something ridiculous with it. I decided to go to America and surprise my friends, Ged, Keith and Moira, who were on an exchange trip on their American studies course. I didn't tell anyone. I hitched to London one Friday night and went to Carnaby Street, where I bought 10 pub mirrors, each one 10 by 8 inches, with very British pictures on them. You know the type – Beefeater gin, Rolls-Royce and Bell's whisky. I put them in my rucksack and caught the newly opened tube to Heathrow. Now, at that time Freddie Laker had just announced £100 return tickets to New York, so I bought one. We left at 3pm and arrived at 5pm. I caught a bus into New York. It was November and already night time, and I remember being very cold. My friends were studying in Springfield, so I went to the Port Authority bus station and asked when the next Greyhound was leaving.

'Which Springfield do you want? There are 26 that we travel to from here.' There are probably more. I guess that's why *The Simpsons* chose the name – there is one in almost every state.

I fished out a letter I had from Ged. 'Ohio,' I said.

The next bus was at midnight and I'd already spent nearly all my money. Time to sell some mirrors! I walked to the New York library and set out my wares on the bottom steps by the sidewalk and waited. I was selling them for $10 each and after three hours I'd sold two. I put the rest back in my bag and headed back to the bus station.

The bus was busy and soon we were rolling through the New Jersey Turnpike, heading to St Louis. There was a stop in Harrisburg, near Three Mile Island where the previous March there had been an accident at the nuclear power plant – so I didn't get off the bus. Then another stop in Pittsburgh, where the bus station seemed to be in a very poor area in the shadow of the business district. I didn't feel very safe. Back on the bus, I drifted in and out of sleep until I heard the driver shout, 'Springfield!'

I climbed down from the bus and caught a taxi to the halls of residence of Springfield University. I found the hall that Ged and Keith were staying in and knocked on their door. It was 10 in the morning and they had been out the night before, drinking. They stood staring at me for ages.

'Sorry,' I said. 'Wrong room.' Then I walked off down the corridor. This woke them out of their astonishment and we hugged and laughed and did a crazy little dance. Once I'd explained how I'd got to their door and we had all calmed down, I asked them where we could get breakfast, as I hadn't eaten in 24 hours. They gave me a packet of biscuits and I wolfed them down as they dressed.

It was Sunday, so they knew that Moira would be at Mass, as they were all good Catholics. We went to the university chapel and hid round the corner until just before the service began. Then we crept down the side and slipped into a pew in line with Moira's, with the boys nearest to her and then me. I managed to stay hidden from her view for about 10 minutes and then she saw me and screamed. Right during the lesson. Everyone turned round and we all stared at the ground until the congregation had turned back.

At the end of the service we met outside and went off to the refectory for lunch. It was like something out of *Happy Days* – burgers, hot dogs, fries, brisket and 10 different types of potato. As it was a Sunday, one end of the serving area had been turned into an ice-cream parlour for 'Super Sundae'! I broke one of my maxims in life by eating an amount of food bigger than my head.

The others wanted to know my plans, and I told them I was there for a week. They explained that term finished on the Tuesday and they were going off for Thanksgiving on Thursday. The boys introduced me to their friend Paul Iaffaldano, who lived in Wisconsin, and when I asked if I could hitch a ride and come along with them he kindly said yes. So over the next couple of days I toured the halls of residence selling the rest of my mirrors.

On the Wednesday morning we piled into Paul's huge station wagon and headed north. Our first stop was Kalamazoo, to pick up Paul's sister. America is enormous. As I stared out of the window at the huge farms, laid bare by the coming winter, I realised how small we are on this great big planet. We shared the road with massive trucks and I wondered what it would be like to hitch across the country, following Kerouac's routes. The sky was Eeyore grey and just as gloomy – there was snow on the way. As we came into Kalamazoo University, the sun came out and we passed the huge bowl where the American football team played. We found Paul's sister and she took my place on the back seat, while I climbed into the back with the suitcases. There was just room to lie down in the cramped space. Ged, Keith and I sang 'I've Got A Gal In Kalamazoo'.

We drove on to Chicago where we were going to
spend the night with Paul's grandparents, who lived
in the suburbs to the south. It was dark when we
arrived and we fell out of the car and stretched. We
entered the small detached house and met Paul's tiny
granddad. The first thing he said was, 'I fought against
the English in World War II!', accompanied by a mime
of a machine gun spraying bullets all over the room.
He then spent the rest of the evening staring at us and
talking in Italian to his wife. The only other sentence
he said to us was after dinner when Ged, Keith and
I offered to do the washing-up: 'You break da plate, I
break your face.'

During the night there was a massive snowstorm,
but we helped put the chains on the tyres and
set off. Leaving Chicago, we headed north following
Lake Michigan and past Milwaukee with its
breweries dominating the skyline, the tall chimneys
pumping out steam into the cold November air.
Then on to Oshkosh and up to New London.
We arrived at lunchtime and met Paul's ma and
pa. They lived in a beautiful house in the woods,
the snow on the pine trees making it look like a
Christmas card.

Thanksgiving dinner was at 3.30pm, so to stretch
our legs it was decided we would go for a walk to a
local lake. I'd dressed for my trip in a leather jacket
and I was wearing a pair of Adidas trainers; I was not
dressed as a woodsman. Despite borrowing a pair of

woollen mittens I was frozen in 10 minutes – but I was glad I went. We found deer and then beaver tracks, which we followed to a snow-covered dam. All around it you could see the tree trunks where the beavers had found their building materials. I was now starting to turn blue, so we headed back. We would run on ahead, wait for the others to come down the path, and then kick a tree trunk so that the snow would fall off the branches and cover them.

Back at the house we watched American football until dinner and then we ate, then ate some more, and then, when we'd finished, we ate a little bit more. I've never seen so many vegetables at a home-cooked meal! After dozing for a couple of hours on the couch, Paul suggested we go to a local bar. It was now minus 20 outside, but we jumped in the car and set off.

It was a big bar, by the Wolf River. We played some pool (it was my first game in the States and I couldn't believe how big the balls and pockets were!) and we drank some beers. I hadn't realised that Thanksgiving Day marks the opening of the hunting season and, being a rural community, a lot of locals had spent the day out in the woods. Someone came in shouting, 'Drinks for everyone!' It appeared that he had shot a 12-point stag – the 12 denotes the number of points on the stag's horns.

'Where is it?' Ged and I asked eagerly.

'Outside, tied to the bumper of my truck.'

We ran outside to see, wondering why no one else was interested. Big mistake. It had been warm in the bar, with its three blazing fires, and we had been playing pool in our T-shirts, but outside it was now near to minus 25. We both froze – literally. Neither of us could move and it was impossible to breathe in due to the shock. We had to wait for the others, who, being locals, had gone to put their jumpers and coats on first. They carried us inside and once we were properly attired we went back out. The stag was huge and tied to the front of a utility truck. As the evening progressed, more and more hunters turned up with their trophies. We drank a lot of beer.

On Friday morning, Paul drove me to Oshkosh airport and, with the last of my mirror money, I bought a ticket to New York via Chicago. I spent the night in JFK airport sleeping on the benches, flew back to Heathrow and then hitched back to Liverpool. At college I told them that I had missed the week due to flu – I would have got away with it if one of my fellow drama students hadn't asked me to do a New York accent as I had 'just been there'.

👍

Back in France, I didn't want to put Karen and her new family out, so I left the endless dinner table and stepped outside to find a light drizzle forming a film over everything it touched. The family asked me to stay, but I wanted to head south.

6

Bordeaux

I left Laval at 3.30pm and headed south, reaching Bordeaux at 3am the next morning after four lifts. I'd dozed off on the last lift in an artic and awoke to find myself in the port. I climbed down from the cab and cursed. I had my hammock and needed a secluded copse to hang it, but I was surrounded by warehouses, right in the middle of a big city. I walked about half a mile away from the port and I was so tired (plus the effects of drinking at lunchtime) that I decided to sleep in some tall weeds on a disused wharf. They were about waist-high. I waded into the middle and got out my sleeping bag. I was so shattered that I went straight to sleep.

About two hours later I was rudely awakened by something sitting on my face. My hands were inside the sleeping bag so I shook my head violently to shake my attacker off. There was a screech and then I became aware of things moving all over the sleeping bag. They were rats, about five of them. I screamed and jumped to my feet. When I had finally regained my composure, I packed up my stuff and headed out of the port. It was a long walk to the motorway south and I was still so tired.

I never used to worry about where I slept in those days — I could sleep anywhere. I guess it was thanks to the preparation I'd had in the Scouts. After leaving home, all the flats I'd rented had been very basic — no heating, a mattress on the floor. I liked to feel independent and ready to travel at a moment's notice.

Every summer there was a Scouts' camping competition called the Emlyn. Patrols made up of four boys would have to carry everything they'd need for a weekend camp on a 10-mile hike. Then they had to pitch their tents and build things like tables and chairs using lashings. You would be marked on these, on the food you cooked, how tidy your tent was and how quickly you found your way to the site. I was the patrol leader for Beaver Patrol at Second Cove Scouts. In 1975 we won the Farnborough and Cove competition, which meant I was to carry the Cross of St George flag at the head of the St

George's Day parade the following year. After that, we went to the New Forest and came 11th in the All-Hampshire Emlyn.

It was also thanks to the Scouts that I went on my first trip to America. Three years before my trip to Springfield and Wisconsin I had been on an exchange visit with a troop in Virginia Beach. I'd always been fascinated by America; whenever I was in Queensmead (Farnborough's answer to Westfield), I would go into the travel agents and ask for any new brochures on trips to the USA, which I would pore over religiously. Consequently, I was the first kid in the school to own a skateboard. I also found a huge leather motorcycle glove that I would use as a baseball glove in break-time ball games. I wanted to go to America more than anything.

Then my chance came. John Sherwin, who was in charge of the Venture Scouts in Farnborough and Cove, organised an exchange trip. I couldn't believe my luck. We'd been to Haarlem in Holland the previous year, and I had bent his ear quite a lot about America. But now we were going! I worked at Wickes for six months and then in Waitrose in Fleet to earn the money for the trip. At Wickes I was the Saturday boy, sweeping the warehouse and carrying stuff to customers' cars. At Waitrose, I was in charge of eggs, dairy products and bacon.

On a Saturday we would get a delivery of 48 sides of bacon – 24 smoked and 24 unsmoked. It was my job to slam a meat hook into the shoulder, lift it onto a rail and then push it into a walk-in fridge. The first week I was exhausted by the 36th side of bacon. I was only about five foot two and I had to get a stepladder at first to climb up and sling the hooks over the bar. The steps would be covered in blood from the unsmoked sides, and once I slipped and fell and the bacon came down across me, trapping me in the pools of blood on the floor. The others found this hilarious. I'd have to wear three white cotton coats to stop the blood getting through to my clothes, but this would make me sweat outside the fridge. By the end of the day I smelled like a butcher's jock strap.

Another time when I was working in the summer holidays I'd done all the work I needed to do for my section by five o'clock one Saturday, so I was sent to frozen goods. They asked me to fetch some burgers from the massive freezer upstairs. I walked in and began to gather some boxes together. Outside someone was trying to push a big trolley past the freezer door, and to get past they shoved the door shut, not realising that I was inside. The light went out and I was in pitch-black darkness. I stumbled back through the boxes to the door but the safety bolt didn't work. The freezer had been overstocked during that long hot summer of 1976 and the door had previously been closed against the boxes, bending the bolt and rendering it useless. I thumped and thumped, hurting my hand, but the door didn't open. I shouted but soon realised the futility of this as the door was seven inches thick and made of steel. I was trapped. It was 5pm and the store would close at 5.30 and would not open again till Monday at 9am.

I knew that my only hope was if someone needed something from the fridge in the last half hour of business, but standing there in the dark, gradually getting colder, I thought my time was up. I would be turned into an iceman by Monday, so that if they touched me, I would shatter into a million pieces. I decided to keep myself warm as best I could. I found a large tub of ice cream and lifted it above my head and then back down to my knees. I did this for what seemed like hours. I was now sure that everyone had gone home and I had been left to die. Then suddenly the door creaked open. The guy who opened it had a terrible shock as I ran out, covered in ice crystals, and lifted him off the ground. I was the only teenager in Farnborough that long hot summer to suffer from mild frostbite.

With four months to go before the trip, I was still short of the money I needed, and I was now working six-day weeks at Waitrose. I'll be forever grateful that my mum got a temporary job at Sainsbury's to help me pay for the trip – both my parents were brilliant at facilitating our dreams, and my mum knew how much I was fascinated by the US.

At last the exchange trip came round and we flew to New York. After a night in a New Jersey motel, we took the Greyhound bus to Virginia Beach, a journey that included crossing the Chesapeake Bay Bridge – an amazing structure. We were met by our exchange families and taken to the local naval base, where I remember walking across the huge open space of an aircraft-carrier deck. I also sat in the cockpit of an F-111. We had a week with the families and I managed to play both baseball and American football with local under-18 teams. I was pants in both, although I did hit a single in the baseball game.

The second week was spent sleeping out. Our first trip was to stay on an Indian reservation, as they called them in those days, and I was very excited. But when we turned up, the sight we were met with depressed me immensely. We were to live for two days with the Mattaponi tribe. Eight families lived on this reservation, which consisted of about 10 acres in the bend of a river, and they were self-sufficient, using the land by the river to grow crops. Above this, on an escarpment, were some woods and a museum. It was here that we were introduced to the head of the tribe, a wonderful man who had a big impact on me. His name was Big Chief Custalow Thundercloud of the Mattaponi Indians. (When we passed a Scout badge, he had to sign a form, and he proudly wrote this title in full on each one – it took ages!) He told us that his once proud tribe had been able to ride a whole day and never reach the end of their land, and then he gave us a full tour of the museum. There were animal skins, including two massive bear hides, lots of earthenware pots and flint-headed arrows and spears, and in one corner was a little shop where he urged us to buy presents for our families.

We left him and went into the woods to put up our tents in a clearing around the fire. Greg and I put ours up quickly without fuss and wandered back to the museum. Chief Custalow was sitting on the steps, banging rocks together.

'What are you doing?' I asked.

He smiled. 'Make arrowheads. Do you want to have a try?' He really talked like an Indian from the films I'd seen as a kid. I never worked out if it was just an affectation, but it was spellbinding to us teenagers.

We sat down and he showed us what to do. Soon the other boys drifted over and we were all making arrowheads. He told us to make three each. As we worked, the Chief walked a little way into the trees and began digging a hole. When he came back, he took most of the arrowheads we'd made, leaving us with one each. He then walked over to the hole and dropped the arrowheads into it, covered them over with earth, and trod it down. We asked him why he had done that, thinking it was part of a ritual.

'Well,' he said, 'in a month I will dig up arrowheads. Then take them inside museum. Sell them as 100-year-old arrowheads. Like you buy earlier.' The others were angry but I laughed out loud. He then taught us a snake dance, which he told us was performed before battle. Graham Ide asked him to teach us a rain dance, but he looked up at the sky and said, 'No time now, we must eat.' It was decided that some of us would drive into town and buy pizzas for everyone. We took everyone's order and then John Sherwin said that the Chief might like some. I was despatched to ask him.

'Chief? Would you like some pizza?'

'Yes.'

'OK, what sort of pizza would you like?'

'Pig pizza.'

Apparently, the Native Americans call meat by the name of the animal it comes from – they don't have words like beef or pork. So we bought him a pig pizza.

We spent the second day earning our Native American Scout badge. We made pots and leather purses, which I'm sure turned up later in the museum shop, not that I considered this wrong. It was heart-breaking to see the tribe pinned into this tiny reservation. It was clear to all of us that their lives were a struggle, but the Chief was an optimist and a grifter and he would do anything to look after his people. Obviously, he was putting up with our stupid questions and teaching us in exchange for money for his people. He showed us pictures of himself in full ceremonial outfit with an eagle-feather headdress; he only wore it at Thanksgiving when he took dead game birds to the state capitol to pay the taxes for the year.

Every so often we would ask him to teach us a rain dance, and each time he would give a sideways glance at the sky and say, 'No.' One afternoon we were surprised to find that the leaders had taken down all our tents; this was because the Chief was going to teach us how to build bivouacs. This involved leaning four or five sticks about four feet long against a tree, then taking thinner, whippier sticks and weaving them laterally through the uprights. Finally, we took fern leaves and filled in the gaps to make the shelter rainproof. About halfway through the making of these shelters, the Chief called us to the centre of the clearing where we were building the bivouacs. I looked up above the trees to see dark, gloomy clouds hemming us in.

'Now I teach you rain dance!'

We copied his moves and he chanted in his native tongue – and low and behold, it started to rain. We fell about laughing.

It was only a shower, and once the bivouacs were finished we were sent to the museum to get firewood. The building was raised on brick stilts and underneath there was wood of different thicknesses. We carried it back to the centre of the clearing and the Chief taught Greg and me to build a fire. It was one of the most useful lessons anyone has ever taught me and has come in handy at many festivals – it always works and needs very little tinder. On this fire we cooked burgers and sausages to have with a salad. Then a seven by three foot billycan was brought out, in which there was the biggest blueberry and apple pie – there was enough for all 30 of us. We sang songs and did comic sketches, which the Chief loved. He had a great big growl of a laugh. We asked him to tell us more about his tribe, and at first he told us about buffalo hunts and battles with nearby tribes. Then, at the end of the evening, he asked if we would like to hear a ghost story. Of course we all said yes.

This was his story:

> Centuries ago, my tribe lived in these woods. It was a good time. Many tents, many families. There was good hunting and the tribe lived well. The only bad thing at this time was a great white bear. It terrorised the tribe,

eating a squaw who was out gathering berries, and
chasing off a group of hunters who tried to kill it.
When a boy became 13, like some of you now, they were
sent out alone with a spear and a knife. They could
not return until they killed an animal which they then
presented to the Chief. Now it came to be one boy's time
to prove himself. His mother was distraught, knowing
that if he was sent out alone he would be eaten by the
big white bear. But the Chief made him go rather than
be dishonoured by the tribe.

The boy roamed through the forest looking for something
to kill – a rabbit, a squirrel, anything so that he might
return to his tribe safely. But it was as if every creature
in the woods was hiding from the big white bear. Then
as he sat drinking from the river, he heard something in
the undergrowth behind him.

He grabbed his spear and swung round and there was
the bear charging towards him. In his fright the boy
could not stand, he sat waiting for
the end. The bear leapt and the boy held his spear
forward. It pierced the bear's heart as he fell in a heap
on top of him, killing the beast outright. Eventually
he wriggled out from underneath the animal and made
his way back to the tribe. When they saw that he had
returned empty-handed, the braves teased the boy. But
the boy just stood smiling at them. Then he led the tribe
to the riverside spot where he had killed the bear
and the tribe were amazed. The Chief made him his
honorary son.

*But it is said that the ghost of the white bear still haunts
these woods at night, looking for revenge on the tribe.
Anyone who sees the ghost of the great white bear is
said to die on the spot.*

We thanked him for the story but the mood around
the campfire had changed. He was a very good
storyteller and we were all a little bit scared. He left
us to go back to his lean-to, and we prepared for bed.
We were sleeping two to a bivouac and I was paired
with an American, G. Brad Shaw (yes, his first name
was G, but everyone called him Brad). Eventually we
fell asleep.

We awoke to a terrific noise a couple of hours
later. There were boys running everywhere. Some
had grabbed sticks from the fire and were waving
them around like light sabres (*Star Wars* had come out
that summer) and one boy was standing by his
bivouac screaming. I jumped up and tried to find
out what was going on. At this point the Chief
arrived, laughing his head off. Once he had calmed
us down, he went off into the woods and came back
with something under his arm. After telling the
ghost story, he had made his way back to the museum,
let himself in and got one of the bearskins down
from the wall. He had then gone to his shack and
poured a bag full of flour over the head and shoulders
of the bearskin, creating a white bear. A couple of
hours later he had crept back to our camp and stuck

the head of the bear through the entrance to one of the bivouacs, roaring loudly. The boy who had been screaming had woken up to see the bear's head. The Chief had then run into the woods and occasionally stuck the bear's head out from behind the trunk of a big tree, frightening to death any boy emerging from the shelters.

When the adrenaline subsided we all saw the funny side, but our bivouacs were ruined. The Chief led us back to the museum and we all slept on the floor. We didn't sleep well, though, as we were surrounded by dead animals and weaponry.

The next day we went to a Scout camp by the Potomac River where there were about 200 boys on the site. We played sport and earned badges, including one for survival. We had to go off into the woods and survive for 24 hours, finding our own food. Luckily, we knew how to bivouac. Greg and I set off at 9am and walked about three miles until we found a clearing where there were some animal droppings. We built a shelter and then I made a spear by whittling the end of a stick. We made some snares out of string that we had been allowed to take with us. Then we sat silently and waited to catch something to eat. By nightfall we had still not caught anything and we were both very hungry. Greg had found a patch of wild sarsaparilla and so we made sarsaparilla tea in a billycan. It tasted great! We spent the rest of the night dozing and then waking up hungry and making more tea. At 8am we headed back to the camp – I have never eaten such a big breakfast.

👍

Being able to live rough also came in handy one summer in London. I had been homeless for a month and was sleeping on the street. After my last year at university, I discovered that I'd failed my degree. It wasn't a big surprise – I had missed the deadlines for both my geography thesis (on 'The Development of the Wellington Country Park') and my drama thesis ('The History of the National Theatre's Search for a Home'). Strangely, I wasn't that bothered, but I knew I had let my parents down and felt guilty about that – terribly guilty. When my dad picked me up from Farnborough station that June I cried as I told him. I could see he was angry, and I couldn't blame him, but he told me not to worry. I asked if I could stay with them for a couple of weeks and told him I was going to resit the whole year. In fact, I'd been to a dodgy doctor in Toxteth and convinced him that the reason I had been tardy with my work was the mental anguish of losing my grandmother the previous year. The college had accepted this and had given me permission to resit, but obviously I wouldn't get a grant.

I decided that I would sign on the dole and live on that while I resat the year. My dad was furious – he had never signed on in his life, and nor had my mum. They thought I should get a job, but with 3 million unemployed that summer, I figured that there were more deserving recipients of work than me. I pointed this out and said I would be quite happy to live on the £17 a week the dole paid. We had an argument – quite a big one. I'd already been to the DHSS in Farnborough and had given my parents' address as mine. They found out when the letter arrived to tell me that I'd have to wait a few weeks for my first cheque to arrive. The outcome of the argument was that I stomped upstairs and stuffed some clothes in a bag, before storming out of the door. I had £2 to my name. I walked to the motorway and hitched to London. The first night was the longest – I had never been homeless before.

I kept moving. Walking for walking's sake, just for something to do. At about 2am I discovered the Barclay Brothers cafe on Whitehall, just down from Trafalgar Square, and I was drawn in. It was brightly lit and full of all sorts of night owls: there were homeless people like myself, clubbers, policemen, and a few sensational drag queens in six-inch heels and big blonde wigs. I bought a coffee and sat in the corner. I took out the Kerouac book I had grabbed as I left the house, but I was too tired to read it. I made that coffee last nearly three hours and no one bothered me, although some people did talk to me and the drag queens entertained me and shared their cookies (not a euphemism). Over the next three weeks I visited the cafe almost every night – it was my safe place. As the sun started to come up that morning I headed to the South Bank. My study of the National Theatre meant that I knew the building well, so I would wait until it opened and then find somewhere on the upper floors to have a nap.

I took the long route there to waste some time. I went down to Parliament Square, across Westminster Bridge and then along the walkway towards Waterloo Bridge. On the grass, just along from where the London Eye is now, there was an exhibition of bus shelters. There were about 60 of them – all different shapes and sizes sent from county councils all over the country and a few from abroad. A few homeless people were packing up their stuff and moving on, but I decided that this would be a great place to sleep for the next couple of weeks.

So the following night I arrived at around midnight and picked one of the empty shelters. I was only able to grab four hours of broken sleep, but it was better than the night before. My money was running out, though, and I had to find a way of getting food. In the morning the two guys in the bus shelter next to mine came and asked if I had any tobacco. I told them I didn't smoke, but then we got talking and I discovered that they had buddied up on the street. They were both about 20 years older than me and neither had had a chance to bathe recently. One was called Bob and came from Liverpool, and the other was Barry from Leeds. I told them I was hungry and asked them what they did for money. 'Panhandling,' they told me. They were both looking me up and down like I was a turkey in a butcher's shop window on Christmas Eve.

'He'd be good,' said Bob.

'Might be perfect,' said Barry.

'Come with us,' said Bob.

We gathered up our belongings and walked to Waterloo station. It was 7.30 in the morning and the commuters were already pouring off the trains and out through the exits. We positioned ourselves at the top of the steps by the War Memorial, against the wall. They would describe someone in the crowd coming towards us and push me forward. I had to say to whoever they picked out, 'Excuse me sir/madam, but could you spare some change please? I'm trying to get home.' Nothing more, nothing less. They told me to look into the mark's eyes as I said it. I don't know exactly what sort of person they were looking for, but I had a 95 per cent hit rate. It was amazing – in 20 minutes we had £2.

'Right,' I said. 'Who's next?'

'No one,' Bob replied. 'We're off now.'

'What?' I asked.

'We've got enough now.'

I followed them down the steps and round the front of the station to a small supermarket. We went to the back and they found what they were looking for: a cheap bottle of sweet sherry that cost £1.89. They gave me the change – all 11p of it. We walked down Waterloo Road to The Cut and sat on one of the iron benches in the gardens opposite the Old Vic. The boys drank their sherry but I didn't want a drink. I pointed out that in future I should get a third share of our successes, and after a short argument they agreed.

They began to tell me their stories. First, Bob showed me his arm. There was a scar running the length of it and a big dent on the back. He told me he had been in the army and had fought in Korea. A bullet had hit him just above the wrist, had travelled along his arm and then had exited where the dent was. He told me that he had seen horrible things, and when he came home he couldn't deal with life outside the army. His wife had left him over his drinking and had taken their two kids. A judge had awarded her the house and he had gradually drunk more and more, losing everything. Barry had got divorced first and then had started drinking. They both claimed they were happy on the streets and that the two main reasons were that they hated filling in forms and didn't like having to do what they were told. They called themselves the Kings of the Road. We returned to the station for the evening rush hour and this time grifted for about 30

minutes. I made a pound. I remember it so well –
buying a cheese and pickle sandwich and how good
it tasted.

This was our weekday routine but on Saturdays we
went to the Strand and hit on the people emerging
from the two theatres there – both matinee and
evening. On Sunday we sat on the path by the Thames
and the 'Kings' told me which of the tourists to ask.
They were unerringly correct in their choices. When
they were drunk, they finally told me that they were
using me because I looked lost and younger than my
21 years.

One Monday morning I had a life-changing
experience. We had panhandled during the morning
rush hour and were sitting on our usual bench opposite
the Old Vic. I was watching the world go by when
I suddenly noticed an angular old man with swept-
back grey hair and small round spectacles. I recognised
him immediately – it was Samuel Beckett. I couldn't
believe it. Bob and Barry were less impressed and more
into the sherry bottle they were sharing. I jumped up
and followed Mr Beckett, in my opinion the finest
playwright of the 20th century. He headed down The
Cut, striding out with his long legs. I realised he was
heading to the pub opposite the Young Vic. It was just

BECKETT
DIRECTS
BECKETT

Photo: John Minihan

The San Quentin Drama Workshop

AT

THE YOUNG VIC

29 July - 9 August

after 11.30 and I caught up with him as he waited for the landlord to unlock the door. Once it was open we both walked in and up to the bar.

'What can I get you?' asked the barman.

'A large dry sherry,' said my hero.

When the barman returned with the glass of sherry (probably the same sherry my friends were enjoying up the road), I plucked up the courage and said, 'Please, Mr Beckett, it would be an honour if I could buy this drink for you.'

He nodded, picked up the drink and headed to a corner table. I had just enough money left to order a half of lager, so I paid and followed Sam to his table. He had taken off his trench coat and had hung it on the back of the chair next to him. As I sat down opposite him, he took a copy of *The Times* from his coat pocket. Then, as I was about to ask my first question, he flicked the paper open and held it at arm's length, touching the table top and creating a wall between us, silencing me perfectly. I picked up my glass and moved to another table.

Two weeks later, when I had cashed my first dole cheque, I bought a ticket to see a double bill of *Endgame* and *Krapp's Last Tape* performed by the San Quentin State Prison theatre company and directed by Samuel Beckett at the Young Vic. It was an amazing night of theatre and it led to me choosing to do my own version of *Krapp's Last Tape* for my drama resit. But I never resat my exams – by then I was already performing my poetry and figured that I didn't need a piece of paper to prove anything.

👍

But, for now, I had a long walk across Bordeaux to the road south to Spain.

7

Biarritz

I arrived in Biarritz late in the afternoon, walking into town from the motorway. It was a hot day and I couldn't wait to take my rucksack off. I made my way down to the beach and was struck by the beauty of the place. The main beach has cliffs at the top of which, at the south end, sit hotels, shops and restaurants, with the path down guarded by the imposing building that is the casino. At the north end is the palace that Napoleon built for Josephine. It has 365 rooms and is now a posh hotel. The promenade is wide and the beach is covered in a fine, pale-yellow sand. It's a great surf beach – world-championship events are held there. There is also a large rock with a small Christian shrine that is linked to the road to the fishing harbour by a small iron bridge. The view is stunning and I fell in love with the place.

Just in front of the casino, a group had gathered on the beach: there were two Swedes – Pella and Stefan – an American called Cabot, and a German girl called Martha. Pella had a guitar and was singing Beatles songs with a strong Swedish accent. A bottle of red wine was being passed round. I introduced myself to them and asked if they would watch my stuff, and then I ran into the surf. It was fantastic. I bodysurfed on a few waves, then made my way back up the beach, where Stefan offered me the bottle to take the salt taste from my mouth.

They told me that they were sleeping on the beach – all except Martha, who was staying in a *pension*. Cabot had been sent to Europe by his father to learn about life before starting university. His dad had given him £2,000 to last the three months, but apparently he had gone straight to Paris, where he stayed in a five-star hotel and ate in expensive restaurants for three weeks until he realised he had only £150 left for the next nine weeks. So he'd bought a sleeping bag and a train ticket to Biarritz. Like myself, he had heard of the place from F. Scott Fitzgerald and Hemingway novels. He was now living on £3 a day, which doesn't sound much but you have to remember that a nice bottle of wine could be had for 30p in those days.

Stefan and Pella had just finished their national service. There was a Swedish school in the town where middle-class Swedes learned French and English in the summer holidays; they had both been to it and had loved their time there. They were good surfers and Pella had represented Sweden in the European Karate Championships – he was extremely fit and couldn't sit still for more than 10 minutes. Stefan was slightly smaller but was better at playing the guitar. He had incredibly blue eyes and all the girls fell in love with him. They both spoke very good English and were very popular in the evenings with that year's bunch of students from the Swedish school.

Martha was 20 and had short, dyed-red hair. She had broken up with her boyfriend of five years and had booked a month in Biarritz during her university's summer recess. Her English was minimal, except when it came to song lyrics. Cabot was madly in love with her, but I don't think she was as interested in him. The Swedes and I had great fun watching their love bloom and then fade over the next fortnight.

They accepted me straight away. We were joined by others, usually Interrailers, for the odd night, but this was the core group. I was the oldest at 22, and quickly became very protective. The first thing they told me was: 'We are at war with the local police chief.'

We never learned his name, but he hated us. He called us 'bums' and tried to make our lives hell, but each time we had the last laugh. It was like *Hogan's Heroes*. He was about five foot four inches tall and was preceded by his beer gut. He had a very Gallic moustache, too. His sidekick was a young skinny lad, about our age, who never said anything and stood with his hands in his pockets, staring at the ground as his boss berated us. I think he would rather have been hanging out on the beach with us. The police chief's main gripe was that we made the beach look scruffy, so our first plan was to tidy the area around us. This is when we found out that you got a franc for each pop bottle returned to the nearby supermarket. (It's probably time we went back to that system to decrease the number of plastic bottles.) At the end of each day as the sun was setting we'd all go off and collect the empty bottles along the whole beach. It would take 30 minutes and we usually found about 25 bottles, with more at the weekend. They were litre bottles and chunky. Once we had gathered them up, Pella and I would take them to the *supermarché* and use the money to buy baguettes and bottles of cheap wine, plus some ham or cheese and tomatoes or lettuce. Then, as the sun set, we would sit and sing and get slowly drunk, together with anyone else who wanted to join in.

There was one person who joined us every evening, but it took us two days to actually get him to sit with us in our circle. He was incredibly shy, but at six foot four it wasn't easy for him to hide. He was 18 and Basque and his family were shepherds high in the Pyrenees on the Spanish side of the border. He had been called up for his national service but didn't want to go. We learned this through a young Spanish girl who managed to get him to open up. We asked his name but he didn't want anyone telling the police. He was very scared of the police chief and changed his sleeping arrangements after he was woken up by him one night. He would disappear at two in the morning and return the following evening. After about 10 days I found him in the tunnel under the cliffs by Napoleon's hotel when I was on one of my constitutionals – it appeared that this was where he went to sleep each night. A more gentle giant I have never met. With his size and silence he reminded Cabot and me of the Native American in *One Flew Over The Cuckoo's Nest*, so we called him Wrigley's. Every Saturday his dad would drive over the border with a parcel of food and a small sum of money for him to survive on. I often wonder what became of him.

At around one or two in the morning we would climb into our sleeping bags against the promenade wall and fall fast asleep. The first night I slept there, I had a very rude awakening. The police chief had obtained a hose that they used to wash the promenade free of sand. He crept up to the edge of the wall, told his assistant to turn on the tap, and then sprayed us all until we ran down the beach with our soaked sleeping bags. It was 7am! We cursed him and he told us that he was just cleaning the promenade and then drove off laughing.

We sat on the beach and planned our next morning's response. Cabot had an alarm clock, so he set it for 6.50. When it went off, we all struggled out of our sleeping bags (which had dried in the sun the day before) and packed them away. When the police chief turned up, we were all sitting on the edge of the promenade, singing 'The Sun Has Got His Hat On'. He seemed pleased that we weren't cluttering up the beach but disappointed that he wouldn't be able to drench us again. He drove off towards the little harbour and as he disappeared from view we all cheered and flicked the finger in his direction. After 10 seconds his car reappeared as he reversed back again, and we all turned our gestures into waving. We then jumped back onto the sand and got into our sleeping bags again so we could grab another couple of hours' sleep until it became too hot in the sun. We did this for the next two weeks, and he was completely unaware of what we were doing.

I had already had some run-ins with the police in Liverpool. For some reason, it was thought to be a badge of honour to have a police record among the lads at college. It was never for anything serious – stealing a pub ashtray, cycling without lights, minor shoplifting. I received my criminal record in my third year at college. It was September, the start of a new academic year. As there were only 30 lads at the college we tended to stick together, and at the start of every term we would have a pub crawl called the Andy Capp Day. The first one of the year was also an initiation for the freshers. The crawl would run from noon till 10.30pm and we would assemble in the student union all dressed in jeans and jackets, with a flat cap on our heads and a copy of the *Daily Mirror* in our back pockets. If you were caught without either your flat cap or your newspaper you had to drink a shot of whisky. We would have a pint in the college bar, then head down Mount Pleasant to the big Yates's Wine Lodge, where everyone had a dock (half a pint) of Aussie White. We would work our way via two more pubs to the Pier Head, where we would catch the ferry across the Mersey to Birkenhead and have a couple of pints in the pub next to the wharf (where I was banned for playing 'Pearl's A Singer' four times in a row on the juke box), staying there until it closed at three. Then it was back on the ferry. On reaching Liverpool, we would head up the hill to the Liverpool Polytechnic student union, which was the only bar open between 3am and 5.30am in those days – they had a special licence.

Here, the freshers would have to drink a yard of ale. The yard glass was kept on two hooks over the bar and it was my job as secretary of the Andy Capp Society to climb up and get it down and then fill it for each of the initiates with whatever beer they had chosen. Drinking a yard isn't easy: first, a yard contains three pints; and second, there's a trick to it. As you drink

more beer you raise the bulb higher, but if you don't
turn the glass constantly as you drink, air suddenly
rushes into the bulb at the end and a wave of beer
rushes towards your face. Of course, none of us told
the newcomers this – just as no one had told us – and
they would end up confused and soaked. Some people
were naturals at it but most gave up after a pint.

I decided to have another try that afternoon. I filled
the glass with three pints of the flattest bitter on offer
(I'll never forget Michael Boggan attempting to do
it with Guinness, which is way too heavy a drink).
The first time I'd tried in my first year I had managed
only two pints before stopping, but that afternoon I
finished the whole yard in 27 seconds! The boys went
crazy. But about 10 minutes later the alcohol hit and
the whole day got a bit foggy.

As I was the club secretary I had to keep a record of
all that went on in each pub we stopped at. Next up
was Rigby's – or Rigsby's, as Tony Wretham dubbed
it after Leonard Rossiter's character in *Rising Damp*.
We then went to The Grapes on Mathew Street,
where The Beatles used to meet before playing at The
Cavern, and would work our way back through the
city centre, stopping at The Blue Posts, The Central,
The Vines and The Beehive, before climbing Mount
Pleasant back to the student union.

When we got to The Central, I realised that I had
left my new jacket at the poly bar – it must have been
the yard! I told the others that I would catch them up

and headed back towards the river. I reached the bar and recovered my jacket, but then decided to take a shortcut back, across the inner-city motorway. I had just returned from Interrailing, during which I had been to my first bullfight. In my paralytic state I began to bullfight the speeding cars with my jacket; I know this because my actions were spotted by two plainclothes policemen in an unmarked car. They pulled off at the next slip road and walked back. I had climbed over the fence by now and they watched as I took out a biro and wrote something on a Buzby poster (Buzby was a cartoon character in a campaign for British Telecom that year and was voiced by Bernard Cribbins in the TV advert). They approached me from behind, and as I finished writing my name on Buzby's yellow T-shirt they tapped me on the shoulder. I spun round, nearly falling over in the process because I was so drunk. The older of the two produced his warrant card and said, 'Police.'

Now, a couple of weeks before, James Kelly had been found dead in police custody, so when I found myself before two plainclothes policemen, in my drunken state I decided it would be very funny to cower with my hands over my head and shout, 'Don't hit me! Don't hit me!' – which they obviously didn't find funny at all.

'Why are you defacing this poster?' asked the one in charge.

'What?' I said indignantly.

'Why have you written your name on this poster?'

I looked at where he was pointing and saw my name on Buzby's T-shirt.

'Because I am a drama student, and it is my aim to draw attention to my name,' I replied.

The next thing I knew I was being bundled into the back of the police car and driven off to Station A. That was my first and only night spent in a police cell and I have no wish to repeat it. Once the paperwork was done, I was led down to below street level and put in a room eight feet by five. There was a stone bench to sit and sleep on and a metal bucket in the corner.

'You stay there until you've sobered up,' said the policeman who had booked me. 'We're going to check that you live where you say you do.'

I lay down on the bench. I was sobering up fast and after an hour I told them I was ready to go home, but apparently that isn't how it works. Two days earlier I had moved into digs for the year. I had a room in a terraced house, run by a 60-year-old churchgoing lady who lived on the ground floor. It was very cheap – £30 a month – but the landlady had impressed on me that she only wanted students who were well behaved. It must have come as quite a shock when two police officers turned up at two in the morning to ask her if this was in fact my place of abode. The police released me at six, and when I walked through the door of my lodgings an hour later she informed me that I was no longer welcome there.

I found a flat a couple of days later and received a letter a week or two afterwards summoning me to Liverpool magistrates' court. On the day I put on my best jacket, a smart shirt and a clean pair of jeans and, not having any money, I walked the three miles into the city, a bag of nerves. I was shown to the waiting area and waited to be called. After an hour my name was read out and I was ushered into the courtroom, where I was shown into the dock in front of three magistrates. There were two women flanking a very stern-looking man, all of them in their 60s. They presided over the court from high-backed oak chairs. As I climbed the two steps to the dock, a cheer went up behind me.

I turned round to see where it was coming from. Above the door I'd come in through at the back, on a wide balcony, sat about 30 of my fellow students from Notre Dame. They were grinning like idiots and giving me the thumbs up.

'Silence in court!' the magistrate in charge shouted. Not a good start – and it got worse.

'Call the arresting officer.'

A policeman entered the courtroom and took the stand opposite me. He held a notebook from which he read out my case, describing my bullfighting the cars and writing my name on the poster. The charge was drunk and disorderly behaviour and criminal damage. The magistrates conferred and then I was asked if this was a true summary of events. I nodded.

Turning to the police officer, the head magistrate asked him to explain what exactly the criminal damage had involved.

'The defendant wrote his name on a Buzby poster. When asked why he had done this the defendant replied, "Because I am a drama student and my aim in life is to bring attention to my name."'

This brought howls of laughter from the balcony, and a few cheers too.

'Silence in court!'

The woman magistrate on the left then explained who Buzby was.

'Did you write on the poster?' I was asked bluntly.

'Yes, Your Honour, I did, in biro. I doubt if you could see it from the other side of the road.'

'You will address me as "Your Worship", I'm not a judge – yet,' he quipped, but nobody laughed. 'Is this true? The defendant used a ballpoint pen?' he asked the policeman.

'Yes,' came the reply through gritted teeth.

The magistrates conferred. They worked out that the poster was made up of eight panels and that the advertising hoarding cost £16 for a week. As I had damaged only one of these panels, the damage I had done was worth £2.

'Do the police really think cases like this are worth bothering the court with?' he asked the copper. The policeman looked suitably admonished. Then the magistrate turned to me.

'As for you, I would encourage you to spend more time on your studies than in pubs! I hope you have learned your lesson. You are bound over to keep the peace. If you are brought before the court again within five years this case will be brought against you at that time. You are to pay £2 damages which will be sent to the owners of the advertisement hoarding. Do you have £2?'

'No, Your Honour – I mean Your Worship. Sorry.'

'Is there someone here with you who could pay your fine?' he inquired.

'I can, sir!' came a shout from the balcony.

Quick as a flash I stepped down from the dock and stood below the balcony edge, my hands cupped to catch the rain of falling coins from above. I missed a few, which disappeared under the furniture. The magistrate was banging his gavel and shouting for order. It was chaos. Eventually, though, I managed to collect the £2 I needed and approached the bench, holding it before me. I gave it to the court clerk.

'You are very close to a charge of contempt of court. I suggest you leave immediately and do not return if you know what is good for you!' the magistrate said angrily. Thankfully, that was my first and last time in court as the defendant.

Back in Biarritz it was the morning of my birthday and Pella and Stefan had bought a bottle of cheap champagne to celebrate. We had it for breakfast and then I headed off to the station to catch the train to Bilbao for the England v. France football game.

8

Bilbao

As I said, England were due to play France on my
birthday – 16 June – just across the border in Bilbao.
I'd decided to treat myself and go to the game. I left
my bag in the left luggage at Biarritz station and
caught a train to Bilbao. There were a lot of England
fans in town that day and this was at the height of
football hooliganism. The fans I saw were the worst
sort – thugs, hell bent on causing trouble. There had
been running battles with police near the old port and
I stayed well out of it, but because of this day I have
been to only one England game abroad since. (That,
unfortunately, was England v. Tunisia in Marseille in
1998 – another embarrassing day for English football.)

If it were down to me, I would take their passports
away and never let them have them back. I know there
are England fans who go to games and learn about

the city they are travelling to and try the local food and culture. I'm not talking about them – I'm talking about the ones who still sing 'No surrender to the IRA'. The ones who do Nazi salutes. The ones who travel without tickets and who trash bars. I follow England at every tournament, but I won't go to the ground to watch them play.

Unless you witnessed it, you can't appreciate how bad the football hooliganism of the late 1970s and early 1980s was. Football was much more tribal and each club had its 'firm' that dished out random violence to visiting fans or took it with them to away games. You knew which games would be trouble, but each team could bring menace. I'll never forget an Aldershot v. Bournemouth game when Bournemouth was in the Fourth (now Second) Division). Ged Smith caught the brunt of the hooliganism that day. It was half-term and we decided to go to my parents' for a couple of days. I'd phoned my mum and warned her.

We left Liverpool after a party on the Thursday night at about 11pm – I'd worked out by then that the quickest way to get to London by hitching was to go at night. There was hardly any traffic on the roads so you travelled faster, and also people wanted the company or they wanted someone to keep them awake. Well, the lift we got that night was definitely in the second category. It was an artic lorry driven by a Scouser who had just picked up at Liverpool docks;

we were ecstatic as he was going to London. We climbed up into the spacious cab where there was a passenger seat and behind that a bed where he obviously slept. He told us that he'd been out with his mates all day and was feeling a bit tired, and he had only picked us up to keep him from falling asleep. All went well until we got to Stoke, when I noticed that his eyes kept closing. I shouted at him and he woke up. I suggested we stop at Keele services as he clearly needed a coffee.

Back on the road he seemed fine – the driver and I argued about football, with Ged half asleep on the bed behind me – but the nearer we got to London, the worse he got. He refused to stop again as he wanted to do the whole trip in one. A new law had come in that meant each commercial vehicle had to be fitted with a tachometer that recorded when the lorry was moving and at what speed, and his boss would see the disc. He then did something I wasn't expecting: he slid the window open and shoved his head right out, the cold October air smashing him in the face and waking him up. Somehow we got to the end of the motorway and he dropped us at Brent Cross. We got the first tube to Tottenham Court Road and had breakfast in the Golden Egg. We then took another tube out to Richmond, arriving in Farnborough at 9.30 and going straight to bed.

That Saturday Farnborough were playing away, so Ged, Neil (my brother), Pete Carey and I caught the bus over for the Aldershot v. Bournemouth game. We saw the comedy actor Arthur English at the turnstile as we went in, although he refused my request for an autograph. Even at this level there were thugs who would go to the game looking for a fight rather than to watch the football – probably not Arthur English, though. Ged and I had been to Liverpool v. Manchester United a couple of weeks before and had seen the ugly side of football when hundreds of fans had fought a pitched battle outside Anfield. We knew how to look after ourselves but I usually felt safe among the Aldershot fans – Aldershot was an army town and home of the paras. The only time it didn't feel safe was when they were playing Hereford, who would bring a load of SAS who would spend the game fighting with the paras.

Aldershot v. Bournemouth was Mickey Mouse football. Aldershot won 2–0 and we started to make a move. We were told that the Bournemouth fans were waiting at the Clock End exit, so we left at the other end. When we got out, we turned left down the hill to go to the bus station and suddenly a dozen Bournemouth fans came running up the hill chased by three coppers. We pushed in against the railings in order to let them past but the first one punched my brother's ear in front of me. I ducked, and the next thug headbutted Ged directly behind me. He caught it square on the jaw and down he went. Pete had seen all this and was down on his haunches, cowering. The rest passed us, swinging punches, while I tried to cover Ged with my body as he was in a lot of pain. It all happened so fast. The police called for an ambulance – the bastards had broken Ged's jaw. I felt awful. He was in hospital for two days and missed a few lectures, and I hitched back on my own.

In November 1980, Farnborough Town made it through to the first round proper of the FA Cup and were playing away against Yeovil Town. I hitched down from Liverpool on the Saturday morning, leaving home at 5am, and just made it to the ground for kick-off. I found my mate Pete Carey and his brother Martin among the Farnborough fans. The match was a turgid affair played on a cold, windy Somerset afternoon and the famous sloped pitch was cutting up after three days of rain. Both sides cancelled each other out for most of the first half, but, just before half-time, Yeovil scored from a corner. We had a Bovril and tried to keep warm.

The old ground at Yeovil had covered stands on only three sides; the other side was an open terrace behind the goal that Farnborough was now kicking towards. Because of the rain, it was empty, but due to youthful enthusiasm I thought that Pete, Martin and I should brave a soaking and go and stand there. It must have looked pretty funny to the Yeovil fans at the other end, all dry and cosy. We walked three-quarters of the way up the terracing and when there was a

Farnborough attack we would spill down the terraces as if we were standing on the Kop at Liverpool. We sang songs and generally dicked about until the unbelievable happened – Farnborough equalised! We went mad, running around like maniacs, throwing our hats in the air and celebrating with the team behind the goal. It was wonderful. We no longer felt the rain. We laughed and sang as loud as we could.

This was too much for some of the Yeovil fans. I noticed it first. To our right there seemed to be something happening at the far end of the stand near the Yeovil end. Something was moving down the stand towards us – it was like a really slow Mexican wave. The crowd was parting to let a group of lads through, and just after they reached the halfway line I could make out why. There was a gang of skinheads with white and green scarves – the Yeovil colours – marching purposefully towards us. I would say there were 15 of them, aged from 13 to 19.

The three of us started to move along the terrace to the corner, where we encountered a three-foot wall. At this point the skinheads reached the other side of the terrace that we had been on, breaking into a trot on its wide open spaces. We hopped over the wall and made our way along the sparsely populated open part of the side stand, but when we reached the halfway line our path was blocked by the wall of the players' tunnel. It was too high to get over but there was a policeman standing in the tunnel mouth.

'Hello! Excuse me! Hello,' I pleaded.

He completely ignored me and turned his back on us. This was the point when the skinheads reached us. Pete was up against the wall and Martin and I in front of him as the blows rained down. I turned round to face them, using my bag against the punches, although a few still got through. (I had my bag with me as I was going to catch the supporters' coach back to Farnborough to see my family.) I was shouting at them to stop and a few old guys in the seats above us joined in, telling their lads to back off. The policeman was still looking the other way. The whole mêlée probably lasted only 20 seconds. Pete and I were all right, just bruised, but poor Martin had his nose broken and a split lip too. I was furious. I rolled Martin over the wall onto the side of the pitch and demanded that the policeman find him medical help. I still can't believe his behaviour, which might explain the mistrust I felt towards the police at the time.

Martin was taken down the tunnel by the Yeovil physio, who convinced a club official to take him to the local hospital. Pete and I were taken to a bar where another club member apologised and bought us a pint. We asked how long it would take for Martin to be fixed up as we were catching the supporters' bus, so the guy went off to find out. We heard a cheer from outside and knew in our hearts that Yeovil had scored. The supporters' bus departed without us but the Farnborough directors came into the bar and said we could travel back with them on the team coach. The players came into the bar for a pint and we were introduced to everyone. Pete and I had pints bought for us and they even waited for Martin to come back from the hospital. He had seven stitches in his lip and had been given strong painkillers, and the three of us climbed onto the coach in a daze.

Back in Bilbao, I headed to the ground and went in search of a ticket. In a tiny bar within sight of the main stand of the San Mamés stadium I found an old Spaniard with 10 tickets for sale. I paid him roughly £5 for one. I told him it was my birthday and showed him my passport as proof, and he bought me a beer and introduced me to some friends of his. He wouldn't let me buy him a beer in return but kept them coming till 15 minutes before kick-off. I crossed the road and saw that the queue to get into the ground was massive, so I started walking along to find the end. The fans were squashed onto the six-foot-wide pavement against the wall of the stadium. I'd walked 20 yards when I saw why the fans were hugging the wall: the police, who were standing at 10-yard intervals, had been issued with electric cattle prods and every time a fan stepped onto the road they would jolt them back into the crowd.

I suddenly noticed a cattle prod coming towards me. Just in time, a hand came out of the crowd and dragged me up onto the pavement. The prod hit the guy next to me and everyone touching him screamed. A lot of people were cursing me, but I'd got into the front of the queue. We made our way through some very old turnstiles and climbed the stairs at the back of the stand. As we came through the gap at the top of the stairs, we saw Bryan Robson score England's first goal after 37 seconds. We spilled down the terrace into the middle of the madly celebrating England fans. France came back and Gérard Soler equalised after 25 minutes. It was a pretty even game, but after half-time England took control. Robson scored a second and then Paul Mariner made the game safe with a third. We sang our hearts out. It was probably the best birthday present I had had up to that point.

After the game I discovered that I had lost my return train ticket to Biarritz and so I had to hitch back. I eventually made it back at about 4am, but the station was closed and so I couldn't get my stuff from the left-luggage office. I spent a cold, damp night waiting for the station to open.

My love of football came from my dad. In his 20s, he'd played semi-professionally for some Isthmian League teams, and he took my brother and me to see our first game in Portsmouth when I was 10. We stood at the front of the stand on a wooden orange box and watched Portsmouth v. QPR. Rodney Marsh was playing, I remember that. At 1–1 my dad decided to leave early, after 80 minutes, to avoid the crush over Jacob's Ladder, a narrow footbridge over the railway lines that run by Fratton Park. The walkways that led up to the bridge on both sides were about 10 feet wider than the bridge, which meant the crowd was funnelled into a narrow gap. As a young boy, I remember the crowd crushing in around me so much that when we reached the first step, as the men went up, I was lifted off the ground and didn't touch the bridge at all on the way across. But as we left the ground there was a loud cheer. QPR had scored. And as we reached the bridge there was another cheer. The game ended 3–1 and we'd missed half the goals. I learned a valuable lesson and always stay for the final whistle to this day.

When I was seven, I had joined the Cub Scouts at Second Cove Troop. I was so excited that they had a football team that I rushed home and told my dad. He took me the following Saturday to Cove Green and dropped me off in the car. When he came back to pick me up, I jumped into the car in an attempt to warm up.

'How was it?' he asked.

'We won 2–1,' I said.

'Did you score?'
'No,' I replied. 'I didn't get on.' He stopped the car.
'You didn't play?'
'No,' I mumbled.

He turned the car around and drove back to Cove Green. He told me to stay in the car and strode off to confront the manager of Second Cove Cubs. Through the windscreen I watched their heated argument as they gesticulated wildly at each other, and then he marched back to the car and angrily drove us home. We walked into the kitchen and told my mum that he was now the coach of the Second Cove Cubs team. It appears he had told the manager that if a boy turned up he should get at least half a game. The guy had told him that he ran the team and would play only the best players, as he was trying to win the league. They had argued about this for five minutes until the other man said, 'If you think you could do a better job, why don't you coach the team next week?' My dad jumped at the chance.

We were a ragtag bunch of tiny lads, playing on muddy, full-size pitches. My dad was true to his word and included everyone who turned up. We still used a laced football in those days, made of leather panels round a rubber inner, which had to be dubbined every week to waterproof it. If they didn't have dubbin applied and it rained, they became heavier than concrete. We rarely got the ball off the ground, but if we did, it was rare for anyone to head it – boys were scared of heading the laced-up opening over the valve as the laces would leave an imprint on your forehead for up to four days. My way round this was to wear a white bobble hat during games that my gran had knitted for me. It cushioned the blow. Of course, whenever we were awarded a throw-in or a free kick, the dads of the opposition team would shout, 'Mark the lad in the hat.' There were no tactics either, and an overhead shot of us on the pitch would have looked like an amoeba's random movements trapped in a rectangle, as all 20 outfield players chased after the ball.

At the age of 11 I moved to a new club, Fernhill Rangers, where there were three others from the Second Cove Cub XI – Robin Gridley, Micky Jower and Graham Fairfield. The rest of the team were in the same year as us at Farnborough Grammar School. We were captained by Derek Lyons, who was the best player among us. We played together for three years, until we had to disband, enforced by the league. The under-13 Farnborough and Cove league was very competitive, but while other teams had improved over the three years, we had stagnated. We didn't have a coach like the other teams but we loved our football – we also had a great team spirit and a great sense of fun.

We played at 3pm on Sundays, all of us cycling to the games. Some games were miles away and we would be knackered by the time we got there. Also, Derek worked in a newsagents at weekends and didn't get out of the shop until two, so when games were far away he would arrive half an hour late. The referees always had a problem with this, as on our team sheet our captain would be one of the substitutes. One of us would play until he turned up and had changed by the pitch, and then he would run on at the first break in play.

That year we were the league whipping boys – we didn't win a game all season and lost most games 10–0. We conceded 128 goals and scored one (in a 2–1 loss to the team that came second bottom). I was playing at centre half and over the season I scored 16 own goals, including a perfect hat-trick in one game (one with my right foot, one with my left and one with my head). Poor old Micky Jower in goal had a thankless task.

The last game of the season was against the team in second place. They needed to beat us 5–0 to win the league on goal difference. The game was in Ash Vale on a balmy day at the start of April and we turned up without a captain. We were all despondent and didn't really want to run out onto the pitch, but then I had an idea. The others made me temporary captain and we sprinted out of the changing block, laughing like idiots. Luckily, I won the toss and we could put my plan into action.

We kicked off and the ball was passed back through the midfield to me on the edge of the area. I controlled it and turned, took the ball to the penalty spot and lashed it into the top corner. Micky Jower did a brilliant dive the wrong way. 1–0. We took the ball back to the centre spot and the ref asked what we were playing at.

'Nothing,' came the reply from our centre forward.

The ref blew his whistle and we kicked off again. The ball went back to the midfield and out to the right back, who dribbled round me and slotted a low shot past Micky, who was hugging the opposite post. 2–0. The other team were now furious. They hadn't touched the ball and they were two up. Some of the fathers were shouting at the ref to do something, but what could he do? We kicked off again and this time Robin Gridley dribbled the ball from the halfway line all the way back to our goal, with two of the opposition desperately chasing him to stop him scoring. He somehow evaded them and scored from the edge of the area. 3–0. We gathered round Robin as if we had scored against the opposing team!

The ref had had enough. He called us to him on the halfway line.

'Are you lads going to take this seriously?'

We muttered a few 'Sorrys' and looked at the ground, but as soon as we kicked off we started to play the ball back towards our goal again. Before we could score, though, the referee blew his whistle. When we stopped, he walked over, picked up the ball and cancelled the match. The dads of the boys from the other team were incandescent with rage as they knew their team needed a 5–0 win. We ran back to the changing room with their shouted insults ringing in our ears. A 13-year-old shouldn't hear language like that!

Looking back now I do feel a bit guilty about taking the medals from those Ash Vale lads, but at the time it felt fantastic.

9

Biarritz Again

The whole time I was in Biarritz, we had only one wet night. The city is situated in the southeast corner of the Bay of Biscay, backed by the foothills of the Pyrenees. Due to its location it can be prone to late-afternoon thunderstorms in the summer, which usually lasted half an hour or so before they blew themselves out and the sun returned to a clear blue sky. But one night at around 11pm we knew we were in trouble. The sky was very dark and over the course of the evening the wind had grown in strength. We gathered up our stuff and headed for the end of the casino where there were arches and a roofed walkway. We were just in time. Out to sea the sky was suddenly lit up by sheet lightning and then came the thunder. The storm was coming straight for us. We sat against the wall, huddled together, under two sleeping bags and my sheet of polythene. Nature provided us with the most wonderful firework display for the next four hours. After that we were too wet to sleep and waited for the following day.

Under the casino, built into the outside wall at beach level, was a public toilet. It was run by a little 60-year-old Frenchman who hated us just like the police chief did. For the first week it was our only option for ablutions. It cost 50 centimes to enter, so we would pee in the sea and only use the toilet for a poo. But then one day Pella took his razor in with him and after he'd used the loo he stood at the sink and shaved. Apparently this was not covered by the 50 centimes and the little guy called the police; the chief came down and banned us from using the toilets. We got round this by waiting for the attendant to go for lunch and then we gave his stand-in a bottle of red every day; he would then let us use the toilets for whatever we wanted as long as we cleaned up before we left.

I filled my days with sunbathing, surfing (we used the extra bottle money at the weekend to hire boards on Monday afternoon), reading and practising my juggling.

I have always liked messing about on water. Even after I drowned. In fact, the experience motivated me to become a very good swimmer to prevent anything like that happening again.

Consequently, when it came to choosing a Cub/ Scout group out of the 10 that existed in Farnborough, I plumped for the 2nd Cove Sea Scouts, which I absolutely loved – especially the camps. We would go for weekends to the Longridge Scout Centre in Marlow, and then for one glorious week each summer we would camp there. I learned to row, canoe and sail over consecutive summers.

Every July they had a regatta. I won races rowing dinghies over 100 metres and sculling a gig (a one-ton boat with 10-pound oars, four rowers and a coxswain). The heats were written on the backs of wallpaper rolls and tacked to the side of a wooden hut. One year I noticed that someone had written something after my name on every sheet – 'A Smart Alec', 'A Smarty', 'A Smart Arse'. Everyone thought it was hilarious. I had an idea who it was: Tuska. He was a member of the local Marlow Sea Scouts troop and the star of the regatta each year.

The finale of every regatta was the BAT polo game between the Hard and the Island teams. BATs were short canoes about six feet long. It was four a side and the idea was to get the ball into the opponent's goal, which was a water-polo goal hung from wires across the backwater. You could use your hands or your canoe paddle to move the ball. It was quite a violent game, as if you reached for the ball with your hand, an opponent could smack it with his paddle blade. The canoes had spray decks on them (a tight skirt with an elasticated edge that clipped over the edge of the cockpit) and so if you got knocked over you stayed in the canoe and either did an Eskimo roll to get back up or waited until a team mate stuck the nose of his canoe in your hand to pull yourself up with. You then had to use your hands like scoops to reunite with your paddles.

We usually reached the final of the event and would inevitably be facing Tuska's team. To be fair, he was amazing. He could travel through the water faster using just his hands than most could with a paddle. I had seen him do 25 Eskimo rolls in a row, and once he did one just using his hands. The power he must have had in his shoulders and hips to even attempt this is unbelievable. He could beat most teams on his own, so invariably we ended up with the silver medal. I had a sort of a love/hate relationship with Tuska, but whether or not he'd written those things after my name, I was determined that he wasn't going to beat me that summer.

The game starts with both teams in line with their goal. The referee then throws the ball into the middle of the river and both teams paddle like mad to get to it. I lined up directly opposite Tuska and, while the ball was still in the air, I was off, paddling like my life depended on it. But I wasn't aiming at the ball, I was focused on the nose of Tuska's canoe. He got to the ball first but, as he reached to grab it, I smashed into the front of his BAT. There was a loud crunch as our two craft collided. I felt water around my feet in the front of the canoe and started to paddle to shore. My BAT was sinking fast. I could see that Tuska was having the same trouble. By the time I reached the side it was almost below the water. Skip Gorvin and Dave Bentley grabbed me and pulled both me and the canoe out of the water. New BATs were being fetched from the racks. But in the five minutes it took to get us back on the water, my team were 2–0 up. The other side were nothing without their champion. Then it was just a matter of parking the ship in front of the tiny goal. They couldn't breach our defence, even with Tuska on their team. We won the game and the gold medal.

The summer camps were halcyon days. We usually camped on a water meadow right by the river between a muddy creek and the boat shed. There were four patrols each in a six-person tent. I was in Beaver patrol (obvs). Each patrol had a cooking tent as well. These had no ends or sides and contained a table, two Primus stoves, a washing-up bowl, some chairs and a hanging larder. The larders didn't contain much: usually just some teabags and a loaf of bread, some butter and a jar of jam. The local swans knew these supplies were there and constantly tried to get at them, and into the stores tent, too. Everyone else was scared of the swans. It was oft repeated that they could break your arm with a flap of their wings. I wasn't scared of them – after all, I had survived death.

If the alarm went up that there were swans on the way into camp, I would grab a tea towel and run to confront them. I would stand tall and flick the tea towel to make a whip-crack noise and drive them back into the water.

The highlight of every summer camp was the trip to Henley for the older boys – patrol leaders and their assistants. Usually they were 17 years old, just before becoming Venture Scouts. It was their chance to get away from the younger boys and get up to some mischief. Due to a rapid rise through the ranks, I had become assistant patrol leader to Paul Sackley at the age of 14. The older boys were not impressed, but they needed me to make up the numbers. There were two groups of five. One group would hike the 12 miles to the campsite at Henley, the others would row up in a gig. We would pitch our tents, cook a meal and sleep the night there. Then the group that had walked up would row back and the group that rowed would hike. I was in the group that hiked there. We crossed the bridge into Marlow and then followed the A4155 through Danesfield. It was a blistering hot day, with a fiery sun burning from a cloudless blue sky. We had packs on our backs, but no one had thought to bring anything to drink. By the time we had climbed the hill up to Medenham we were spitting feathers. There was no shop there, though. In the end I decided to just go up to someone's house and knock on the door. A middle-aged woman kindly brought out a big jug of water with ice and mint in it. Wow!

We continued on our way, but the heat was taking its toll. The road route was 12 miles, the river route eight. When we finally reached the farm field where we were camping the others had arrived, put up the tents, dug a fire pit and started cooking. Being youngest I was given the job of digging a latrine. It was a beautiful spot to dig a bog.

We were in a hay field opposite Temple Island, on the north bank of the river, the start point for each race during Henley Regatta. The eponymous temple is a round building with a domed roof, and a couple of years later, a kid we called Captain Scarlet (because he had a lump on top of each shoulder that looked like Captain Scarlet's bleepers) encouraged me to help him row out to the island to steal some lead off the roof. I didn't know what we were going to do with it once we'd got it, but I went anyway, as it sounded exciting. It was the sort of thing that you'd hear in a sitcom at the time: 'They made a fortune from taking the lead off the church roof.' So, after the others had fallen asleep, we rowed out to the island and climbed up one of the narrow Doric columns at the rear of the building and onto the roof. We had a torch with us and we looked around the edge of the roof for any loose bits of lead. Eventually we found a hole. Captain Scarlet grabbed it and pulled, lifting the corner of the lead sheet. Six bats flew out and up into our faces and we fell off the roof in shock, luckily landing on a compost heap below. As we lay there winded, we received another shock, as a light came on! We had no idea that anyone lived there. We ran to the boat and paddled it back to camp.

After we had eaten our Vesta curries (we always had Vesta meals as they were light to carry long distances and very easy to make – just add hot water), the older boys decided to row up to Henley to find a pub. Gary Dutton and I were left in charge of the camp as we looked too young to go into pubs, let alone be served. As a treat, they left us some drinking chocolate, milk and a chunk of cheddar cheese, which we consumed within 10 minutes of them leaving. We kept the fire going for a couple of hours but the heat of the day and the 12 miles we had walked took their toll and we climbed into our two-man tent and fell fast asleep.

We were woken by laughter and shouting and huge flames from the fire pit. The first thing that bothered me was that I was outside my tent, but still in my sleeping bag. The older boys were dancing round the fire hooting like owls. They were very drunk.

'He's awake!' cried Colin Dexter. They all fell to their knees in supplication to me.

'Don't hurt us!' shouted Terry Sloane.

I was very confused. I was still trying to work out how I had got out of my tent in a sleeping bag.

'Are you all right, Andy?' asked Paul Sackley, my patrol leader.

'What do you mean?' I stammered back.

'Oh, you went crazy! When we got back you were standing on the bank, screaming. We tried to calm you down, but you weren't having any of it.'

'Show him the tent,' said Colin.

'Yeah, show him the tent!' chorused the others.

I was led to the six-man tent. There was a massive hole in one of the panels.

'You did that!' Colin told me.

I just stood there, stunned. They told me that they had returned from Henley and were having a quiet can of beer by the fire when I had appeared from the two-man tent that I was sleeping in and charged at them, screaming. They had scattered and I had then picked up one of the heavy gig oars and had tried to attack them with it before using it to make the hole in the tent. They realised that I was doing all this in my sleep. They waited until I grabbed my sleeping bag and lay down next to my tent, then they woke me up.

'Did you eat any cheese before you went to bed?' asked Paul.

'Yes. Yes, I did,' I replied.

'Well, there you go...' said Terry Sloane.

I was horrified. They talked me through it again, then we all went to bed. I didn't sleep too well.

The next morning, the hiking group set off to walk back to Marlow. But not before teasing me about my sleepwalking. We tidied up the campsite and filled in any holes we had made. The older boys were very hungover. They lay in the bottom of the boat, groaning. I was left to row with the stroke oar while one of them held the tiller the other way to keep us straight. After the first lock we hitched a lift from a pleasure boat; they tied our painter (bow rope) to their stern and towed us practically back to Marlow. They gave us orange squash and biscuits and the other boys were enjoying themselves immensely. But I was worrying about what I was going to say to Skip, now that it turned out I was a madman!

When we arrived back at Longridge, the hikers were already there. They must have taken the bus! They told me Skip was waiting for me. I shuffled off and told him what had happened, offering to pay for the tent repair. He was very kind and told me not to worry about it. He could see how upset I was.

About six months later, however, I found out what really happened that night. The lads had rowed into Henley and done a bit of a pub crawl, ending up in a first-floor nightclub where they got into a fracas with some local skinheads. A fight had broken out. They had been chased back to the boat and rowed back with two litres of cider and half a bottle of vodka hidden in the boat, which they tucked into on their return. At first they had kept reasonably quiet, but as their voices became louder and Gary and I didn't wake up, they decided to play a trick on us. They unpegged our tent and lifted it up and over me, then put the pegs back in, so I was outside the tent. Then, as they became drunker, they had decided to have a jousting tournament, which is how the tent had become ripped! That's when they came up with the cheese and sleepwalking story, the buggers.

For years after that, if any of those lads saw me out drinking in the pubs of Farnborough, they would say to me, 'Don't have any cheese, now!'

In Biarritz, Ian MacArdle had taught me the basics of juggling, and now I started working on different tricks. In the evenings I'd stand at the bottom of the steep path from the town to the beach and I'd juggle – with my hat in front of me and Pella or Stefan sitting behind me playing some weird Swedish folk music. People on their evening stroll along the prom would stand and watch, occasionally putting a coin in the hat. I'm sure it was more for the music than the juggling. We would use the money to go to a bar and have a beer and watch whatever World Cup game was on.

Then our lives changed for the better. An American aircraft carrier arrived in Bayonne, just up the coast, on a diplomatic trip. It had been on exercises in the Med and was now on its way home, but the French president, François Mitterrand, had invited the crew to celebrate the 4th of July there.

The first we knew about all this was when a guy with a ladder started putting French and American flags behind the speakers that hung from each lamppost along the edge of the promenade. Then someone noticed a poster for an American film festival at the casino. The films were free to anyone and we went every afternoon. We would take our towels and wash kits and make use of the casino's lavatories, and then wander into the cinema and sit on the front row of the balcony. Due to the great weather and the films all being in English, attendance by the locals was poor. We watched *Gone With The Wind*, *Casablanca* and *West Side Story*. We noticed that in the end scene, when Natalie Wood is cradling Richard Beymer after the big fight, every time it cuts back to them her pendant moves inside or outside her jumper. I can't watch that film without looking for it.

The next unintentional aid to our lives came when the locals built a stage on the beach at the same level as the prom. It was about five feet off the sand and we realised that it would make the perfect shelter to sleep under, so we would wait until 1am and then creep under it with all our stuff. Perfect! Being the oldest and the tallest, I slept on the outside on one side and Pella slept on the other. But on the second night we were attacked.

We were all fast asleep, slightly drunk, but feeling safe in our little shelter. There were six of us: Pella, Stefan, two Interrailing Scousers, Cabot and me. I woke up at around 3am but couldn't move. There was a 30-year-old Moroccan on my chest, his knees either side of my body, trapping my arms in my sleeping bag. His face was about six inches in front of mine and out of the corner of my eye I saw something glint in the dark. It was a knife. I couldn't work out what he was saying, but then I realised he was asking for my money in French. We all kept our money in money belts – which was lucky, as we found out later that they had slit the bottom of our sleeping bags, thinking we would keep our valuables there. Without turning my head I said very firmly, 'Pella!'

There were four assailants. Suddenly all hell broke loose. The Liverpool lads had pushed the guys sitting on Cabot and Stefan into the two who were sitting on Pella and me. Punches were being thrown and there was a lot of shouting. Pella had forced himself up, smashing his guy's head into the underside of the stage, and picked up one of the bottles we'd gathered that evening for its deposit. He ran round the stage to my side and grabbed the collar of my attacker's denim jacket, hoicked him backwards and smashed the bottle over his head. He went out like a light. The other two were trying to beat a retreat from under the middle of the stage while the two Scousers gave them a good hiding. Cabot was yelling that he had been cut. I ran to the seaward side and grabbed his legs and pulled them out. The guy who had been sitting on Pella emerged groggily from the north side and ran off along the beach. The other two were eventually extricated by Pella and me, and after a brief struggle they went running off too. Pella howled like a wolf and beat his chest. The others crawled out and we all went to examine the man who had been coshed with the bottle. He wasn't moving.

'My God, Pella, you've killed him!' screamed Cabot, whose hand was covered in blood.

'Good,' replied Pella, smiling like an idiot.

I bent over him and checked whether he was still breathing. He was. I looked at Cabot's hand, which was cut when he grabbed the blade of his attacker's knife. I sent Stefan with him to make sure he got to the hospital and then I turned back to the Moroccan.

'What if he's in a coma?' I asked the other three.

Pella just picked him up in his arms as if he were a hurt six-year-old and ran off down the beach. I ran alongside him, trying to find out what he intended to do. He ran straight into the sea up to his waist and then dropped the would-be robber into the water. I ran in, too, to see whether the guy was going to drown. On contact with the cold water he came to and struggled against the surf to stand up. Pella ran at him, roaring, and the man sprinted further into the water and began to swim – fully clothed – along the beach. We made our way back to our stuff, which was being guarded by the Liverpudlians. We never saw our assailant come out; he must have swum out to sea, then along and back in at the end of the beach. We had seen this gang watching us for a couple of days, but we had thought they were just checking out how safe it was to sleep on the beach. We didn't see them again.

We sat up, waiting for Cabot to return. He came back at 5am with 22 stitches in his palm. We slept late that morning.

👍

Our shows in the evening were very popular and I'd started telling jokes between songs. I've always had a good memory for jokes since I was little – I'd watch shows like *The Comedians* and *The Wheeltappers and Shunters Social Club* on TV and remember every joke. Now that the town was full of American sailors in uniform I could do jokes in English; my French hadn't been good enough to tell them previously. After the shows, as we drank on the sand, Stefan and Pella would tell me jokes translated from Swedish. This is my favourite one they told me:

Two men are fishing in Stockholm harbour but there's a windsurfer going up and down close to where they are, so one of the men shouts, 'Hey, go away! We are fishing here.'

But the man just carries on sailing up and down
near their lines. So the first fisherman picks up
a rock and throws it at the windsurfer. It hits him
on the side of the head and he falls into the water
and disappears.

His friend says, `Oh, you have killed him. You must dive
in and save him or we will go to prison for a very
long time!`

So he dives into the water, finds the body and drags him
to the quay.

`Oh no!` says his friend. `He`s not breathing. You must
give him the kiss of life!`

So the first fisherman leans over the body, but then
turns his head and says, `Oh, this man has the worst
breath I have ever smelled!`

His friend tells him, `But you must carry on, or we will
go to prison for very many years.`

So he starts to give mouth-to-mouth resuscitation,
but then his friend says, `Wait a minute – this one`s
wearing ice skates.`

You have to think about it. It took me a good two
minutes to get the joke, but then I laughed crazily to
show my enjoyment.

Later that week, we were asleep under the stage when we heard a lot of rumbling and people walking around on it at six in the morning. I looked out to see that four men were pushing a little caravan onto the stage. I ducked back under and told the others what was happening, and we all went back to sleep. Then, at 7am, music started playing from the little tinny speakers hanging from each lamppost along the promenade. We were awake again and the others sent me to find out what was going on.

I climbed out just as the record ended and I saw that there was a DJ inside the caravan talking into a microphone. His words were booming out across the very empty beach. I jumped up onto the stage and walked over to him.

'*Excusez-moi, monsieur.*'

'*Ah, bonjour mon ami,*' he replied, before talking much too fast for my poor French. He could see I was struggling, so he slowed right down and said, '*Où habitez-vous?*'

I knew that one. '*Ici, monsieur! Sur la plage! Mes amis et moi dormir ici sous l'étage.*'

'*Ah. Anglais?*'

'*Oui.*'

'Would you like me to play a record for you?'

'I'd quite like to go back to sleep, mate. I was up drinking your wonderful French wine till three o'clock last night. But if you've got any Beatles, I'll take that.'

I jumped onto the sand and climbed back into my sleeping bag. I explained to the others what had occurred but they had heard the whole thing over the speakers. It was the 4th of July and there were to be a number of events along the beach and throughout the town. The caravan belonged to a radio station and they would be broadcasting all day from the beach. Some 15 minutes later we were dragged out of our shelter by the chief of police. He had been listening in his police car and had heard me say we were sleeping under the stage – he'd been wondering where we were for days. We had thought the radio guy was just warming up, but I had broadcast our whereabouts to him and everyone else within earshot of the beach!

I decided it was time to move on.

10

Lourdes

The Americans and the police chief were spoiling Biarritz for me — it was time to leave and head to Pamplona for San Fermín. I had read Hemingway's *Fiesta: The Sun Also Rises* on the beach and it had piqued my interest. I had a couple of days before the festival started, so my plan was to head to Lourdes and then over the Pyrenees. I'd always been curious about Lourdes, as quite a few of my fellow students in Liverpool had travelled there with their churches. It still amazes me that I never realised Notre Dame College was a Catholic establishment.

👍

When I first went to college, I'd left Farnborough with my red rucksack on my back and wearing a light blue 'Starsky' cardigan, waved off at Farnborough station by my mum and dad, brother and sister. I had caught the train to London, then the tube to Euston, and then a train to Liverpool Lime Street. Excited about this new adventure, I splashed out on a taxi. When I dismounted from the taxi I went through a small gate in a white-painted ivy-coated wall and found myself in the gardens of the halls of residence at Aigburth.

There were nuns everywhere and a couple of priests, too. I wouldn't say that I was anti-religion, and definitely not anti-Catholic – though since I had nearly drowned I hadn't been religious at all – but I was genuinely surprised to see so many nuns. I really hadn't thought about the name of the college and its religious significance. I was that naive!

I was shown to a room on the ground floor of the block called St Mary's. I shared a six-bedroom unit with Tony Wretham, Ged Smith, Mick Boggan, Matthew Battersby, Keith Seed and Paul Rowbottom. Halcyon days! In my first term I noticed that, after tea in the refectory, I would head back to my room and within 10 minutes one of the girls (there were 360 women and 30 men at the college, so we were always outnumbered) would knock on my door with a cup of coffee for me. I was well chuffed by this popularity, but invariably they would turn the conversation round to religion. They seemed amazed that I didn't believe in any religion, let alone Catholicism. I started to get suspicious after 12 similar evenings, so I asked the next girl what was going on. She told me that one of the nuns was upset that I was a heathen, without Jesus, and she had asked the more devout girls to try to convert me. I was flattered that she thought my soul needed saving, but no thank you!

The next night, when my visitor asked me my religion, I told her I was a druid. If she wanted heathen I'd give her pagan. I continued with this line for a week and the visits stopped, but I hadn't quite finished. The last day of that term was 20 December, but most people weren't leaving until the next day as there was a disco to celebrate the end of term. I went to the party and walked home at about 2am from Liverpool.

When I returned to the halls of residence, I crossed the hockey pitch at the back between the building and the railway line. I had spent the previous month collecting sticks on walks round Sefton Park and stashing them behind some bushes by the railway. After a couple of trips I had built a wonderful conical bonfire about four feet high on the centre spot of the hockey pitch. Proud of my work, I returned to my room and waited for dawn. As the sky started to change from black to purple and red, I wrapped the white sheet from my bed around my body and placed a laurel wreath I'd made on my head. I headed out of the back door carrying a bough of holly and a bough of mistletoe.

That winter solstice, the students at the back of the halls awoke to the sight of me dancing round a bonfire, loudly chanting gibberish. I kept it up for about 10 minutes and then retired to my room. If anyone ever asked me what I'd been doing, I would look them in the eye and say, 'Solstice!' They left me alone after that, but it did backfire on me.

One of the drama lecturers, Fred, was Welsh. I was heading into the drama block one afternoon when he grabbed me and said, 'There's someone here I think you would like to meet – you might even know him.' He then introduced me to the chief of the Order of Bards, Ovates and Druids! Fred had invited him to talk about theatricality in ancient rites. I went bright red and mumbled my 'Hello.' There followed a very awkward conversation.

The nuns at Notre Dame were a mixed bunch. My favourite was Sister Mallachy, who was four foot 11 of pure Irish mischief. She was in charge of the sick bay at the halls of residence. I once feigned illness to get out of a test, but Sister Mallachy saw through this. She put me in one of the beds and went to fetch me a cup of tea – a cup of tea that she had laced liberally with laxative. I spent the next day and a half on the loo.

I got my revenge three years later by accident. One summer afternoon, in her role as student welfare officer, Sister Mallachy, together with Sister Mary Donlan, turned up at the terraced house on Garmoyle

Road that I was sharing with Tony, Dean and Steve. Tony, Dean and I were in and invited the nuns into the living room to find out why they had come. They were cycling around student houses to see if anyone was leaving after that term, as they wanted to pass on the landlords' details to those who were about to move out of halls. We asked them if they would like a cup of tea. They said yes, and Dean was dispatched to the kitchen to make it. When he returned, the tea was accompanied by some slices of a chocolate cake he had found in the kitchen.

Just then, Steve arrived home and was shocked to find two nuns in our living room. His face went white when he saw what they were eating and he beckoned for me to follow him into the hall.

'Where did you get that cake?' he asked.

'Dean found it in the kitchen.'

'Shit!'

'What?'

'That's the cake I made this morning. It's got dope in it. What are we going to do?'

'SHERRY!' I blurted out.

I raided the food jar for some money, ran to the corner shop and bought the cheapest sherry they had. Then I ran back and poured two small glasses and gave them to the nuns. If they got a bit stoned, I thought, we could blame it on the sherry. It was a good job I did! Sister Mary Donlan became very quiet and very interested in the pattern of our wallpaper, while Sister Mallachy became the life and soul of the party and started telling us hilarious tales about her Irish upbringing.

There was no way they could cycle back to the halls of residence on the other side of Sefton Park, so we ordered them a cab and decanted them into it with their two bikes. We gave the driver the address and off they went. The next time I saw Sister Mallachy she asked me what type of sherry I'd given her. I told her it was Polish. Whenever I saw her after that we would have the following conversation.

Sister Mallachy: 'And where might you be off to, Mr Smart?'

Me: 'I'm off for a few Polish sherries, Sister.'

I always found it hard, though, dealing with organised religion. I challenged the huge amounts the college spent on its feast day, 6 December. You have to remember the state of the country at the time: the walk from halls to college went through Toxteth, where unemployment was running at 40 per cent. Liverpool was a very poor city in those days and had been ignored by successive governments at a time when container ships were killing off jobs in the port. I argued in the college newspaper, which I wrote, edited and printed, that maybe it would be more Christian to give the money to those in the city who didn't have anything, especially just before Christmas. I was hauled in front of the college board for that one. Their reasoning didn't change my beliefs and I smiled at them throughout the hearing, which I think unsettled them.

👍

In my first year I fell in with four girls in the year above called the Bernies. They lived in a flat over the dairy on Little Parkfield Road, just off Lark Lane. Three of them had the first name Bernadette, the other was a Geraldine, and they were all from Banbridge in County Down. Their parties were legendary and I would call round some evenings for a cup of tea on the way home from the pub. Bernie Mac and I became good friends, although being a good Catholic girl that is as far as it went.

Easter 1978 she invited me to stay with her family, on their farm. I caught the boat from Liverpool to Belfast and then the bus down to Banbridge. You couldn't hitch-hike in Northern Ireland in those days. The Troubles were at their height. In fact, for a naive boy from the suburbs of London, it was a bit of a culture shock. To get to the bus station in the city centre I had to pass through two checkpoints with pat-down body searches. Then as the bus left the city, I saw an armed patrol of British soldiers checking a road of terraced housing. The soldiers looked very tense, but kids were playing on the pavement as if they weren't there.

Bernie met me from the bus at Banbridge and took me home to the farm, which had a dairy herd of about 40 cows. I was made to feel very welcome by her mum and dad, her brother Michael and two sisters. Her dad was especially keen that I should enjoy my stay and we went straight out for a drive round County Down, through Newcastle, Warren Point, Newry and up into the Mountains of Mourne. But everywhere we went he would point out where someone had been killed – a British soldier here, an IRA member there. We stopped on the Newry-to-Banbridge Road. We got out of the car and he told me in graphic detail how the Miami Showband were killed by the UVF at a fake checkpoint. He would point out which area belonged to each side, too. He was very matter-of-fact with these stories of violence and hatred, which I found very hard to deal with. It was just how it was. Everyone in Northern Ireland was living in the shadow of death at that time.

To my naive mind it was crazy for the people of a country to be fighting over two versions of the same religion. I didn't know about the other sides to the argument: the history, the United Ireland claim, the Royalists, the marching, the gangs and the assassins. To think that we are in danger of going back to those days because of Brexit frightens the hell out of me.

I really felt that if I strayed into the wrong area I could be killed for my accent! In fact, that night we went to a local pub and the Bernies told me not to speak as it was in a Catholic stronghold. I did as I was told. Eventually they had spread the word I was a friend from college and OK, and I could join in conversations. But there were still some people in the bar who refused to talk to me. I had a crew cut at the time and must have looked like a soldier to them.

On the second day, Easter Saturday, we went into Belfast, sightseeing. There was a ring of road blocks, checkpoints, barbed wire and turnstiles around the city centre. We went to the dockyard to see where the *Titanic* was built and all around the main shopping streets. Occasionally we would see soldiers on patrol, their rifles slung across their chests. The highlight was a trip to the Crown, opposite the Europa Hotel (still the most bombed hotel in Europe). I had six oysters and a pint of Murphy's and it was heaven. It remains in my list of top five bars in the world.

That night, Michael took me out in the car for a drive. He was a quiet, softly spoken man of 25, very thin with a somewhat haunted look. I knew he worked at the hospital on the Falls Road, but I didn't know what he did there I just assumed he was a junior doctor. We eventually pulled up high above the city on a hill by Hannahstown and I found out why he looked haunted. As we sat looking down at the lights of the city he explained that he worked in the morgue. He opened the glove compartment and pulled out a half bottle of Scotch, then he settled down to tell me about the Troubles whilst we drank it.

Working in the morgue he had seen a lot of horrible sights. Some of the bomb victims that were brought in were in plastic buckets. If there were multiple deaths it was often difficult to know which part belonged to which body. It was his job to try to put together this jigsaw puzzle. He told me how they would use sand in some of the coffins before they were handed over to the families to make up the weight. Every story was heartbreaking.

As we finished the bottle he looked down and pointed out H Block and told me about the dirty protests going on there, led by Bobby Sands. I asked him if there was any way to end the Troubles. He didn't seem to think there was. He said he thought that only about 10 per cent of the population really wanted the Troubles to continue and that 90 per cent had had enough of living in fear. He said that the two sides needed to get around the table and talk, but that it would never happen. I'm so glad that the Troubles have ended. Belfast now is a wonderful city; I have had so many great nights there over the years.

On my last night, Easter Sunday, the three Bernies, Gerry (Geraldine), Michael and I went to the Coach in Banbridge, a massive pub on the Belfast-to-Dublin road. Down one side of the pub was a vast room with a stage at one end. The place was heaving. The early entertainment was a talent show and everyone was going for it as it was a bank holiday the next day. The young people of Banbridge were showing off their singing skills, accompanied by the house band. They all had beautiful voices. After a couple of hours and six pints of Guinness I allowed myself to be coerced into taking the stage. I wasn't going to sing though. I decided to try comedy.

I approached the band and they asked me what song I was going to sing. I told them to take a break as I was going to tell jokes. My accent must have surprised them – they just sat and stared.

I turned to the massive crowd and a hush fell.

'I'm not a soldier!' I blurted out.

There was a long pause. Then brilliantly, the drummer did a rimshot: *bdum-ting*.

There was a huge laugh.

I started to tell old jokes I'd heard on the telly from the likes of Tommy Cooper, Ken Goodwin and Frank Carson. But in my own style. After three minutes, a voice came from the band.

'That's enough.'

I thanked the crowd and returned to my friends. At the end of the contest they announced the winners. I came third and won a bottle of wine. The MC said, 'Look at the balls on this Englishman!' as he gave me my prize. I gave the wine to Bernie's mum for having me, and we travelled back to Liverpool the next evening. I loved Northern Ireland: its people, its culture and its sense of humour.

Now, here I was in Lourdes, to see what all the fuss was about. I found a campsite high above the town, in a forest of pines. I strung my hammock, placed my rucksack in it, and covered the lot with my plastic sheet. Then I headed down into the town. I was amazed at what I saw: every shop was selling plastic figurines of the Virgin Mary – and, of course, Bernadette Soubirous, the local saint who made Lourdes famous. There were crucifixes of all shapes and sizes and made from all sorts of materials, but what caught my eye were the plastic bottles in the shape of the Madonna that were for collecting the holy water from the grotto. The whole experience seemed to be geared towards the locals making money out of the pilgrims.

The queue for the grotto was nearly a mile long, so I made my way round to the other side where people were leaving. I could see in through the exit door – the whole of the ceiling was covered in crutches. But as I stood and watched, people were being pushed past me in their wheelchairs. Maybe it took a while to work! Don't get me wrong – religions can do a lot of good, but this didn't feel right. It felt like a Christian Disneyland, full of promise but really just a big queue.

In the evening there was a candlelit parade through the town, but I decided to give it a miss. Italy was playing Brazil in the final second-league round. As I climbed the hill I heard shouting from a bar and walked straight in. There were about 20 Italian guys watching a big TV, so I ordered a half of beer and sat at the back behind them as the game kicked off.

They were playing at Camp Nou in Barcelona. Brazil, with its team of all-stars, was considered the big favourite to win the tournament and had smashed Maradona's Argentina 3–1 in the first game of the second-round group. Italy, on the other hand, had had a slow start, drawing all three of their first group matches. They had also beaten Argentina in their first match of the group, but only 2–1, so if there was a draw Brazil would go through to the semi-final; Italy would have to win to proceed. What unfurled before us that night was magical. These guys could play. Brazil, with its samba style of quick passing, flowing football, and Italy with its barely legal back four and the rapier thrust of counter-attacking. It is definitely in the top five games I have ever seen.

The Italian men in the bar were very tense before the start and all of them seemed to be talking at once, with no one listening. Some were puffing on cigars, some were drinking small cups of strong coffee. As the whistle blew for kick-off they finally sat in their seats, but they all continued talking. I don't speak Italian, but I could tell from their reactions that a lot of the comments were jokes, some of which were received better than others. A close-up of Paolo Rossi brought a very angry reaction. Obviously I didn't know if he played for a rival club to theirs, or if it was the fact that the Italian FA had knocked a year off his three-year ban for match-fixing allegations. Whatever the reason, he was very unpopular.

Then the first bit of magic occurred. Cabrini floated in a long high cross from the left and there was Rossi in the middle to head it in. 1–0 to Italy. The bar went crazy. I thought these Italian men were loud when discussing the game, but when the ball billowed the back of the net they went mad! There was hugging and kissing and I seemed to get caught up in it. All I did was stand up to see the TV as they all jumped up in excitement as the ball came across. The guy nearest me saw I was standing and grabbed me in a bear hug before dancing me around the bar, my feet off the ground. Eventually we settled back down in our seats. There was a lot going on at the bar. Suddenly six bottles of wine and a load of glasses appeared. These were passed out to everyone and they even placed a half bottle of wine and a glass in front of me. They asked me where I was from, and cheered when I said England. I poured out a glass of wine and raised it to all of them.

Then disaster struck. Socrates played a one–two with Zico and then slid the ball past Dino Zoff. 1–1. The bottle and glass were grabbed from my table and placed back on the bar. Apparently Italians don't drink unless they're winning! I couldn't work out what was happening but I resolved to drink like a fish if they scored again. And they did, and it was that man Rossi again, and I got the bottle back on the table after we had all had another dance around the tiny bar. He had pounced onto a lazy ball across the defence and had skipped round the defender to hit it diagonally across the goal from the edge of the box. 2–1 to Italy. Somehow they managed to hold on until half-time.

Half-time was spent talking to my new-found friends with the few words we shared – mainly the names of footballers we knew. They liked Kevin Keegan, so I told them I was from Liverpool (not technically true, but I had just come from there on this journey). For the rest of the night I was called Liverpool. They were all from a village near Naples and not one of them thought they would stop Brazil from scoring again. I was on my way to being drunk and gave a stirring speech about their team being equally brilliant, especially the defence and midfield. Each time I mentioned a name they gave a cheer. The loudest one was for Gentile.

The second half began and we all took our seats. The tackles were flying in and Brazil's passing was a thing of beauty – they moved up and down the pitch like waves on a beach, occasionally crashing against the rocks of Italy's defence. Sitting in the bar we oohed and aahed and shouted for fouls against the Azzurri (Oscar was putting himself about a bit). But then, just after the hour, Falcão levelled again for Brazil. Back went the wine bottles and glasses. A great foreboding fell over us and there was a lot of wringing of hands. A few of the Italians were swearing at the television.

But then the true miracle of Lourdes occurred: Rossi got his hat-trick. Tardelli hit a shot into a crowded area and Rossi was onside, standing at the edge of the six-yard box. He spun 180 degrees in the blink of an eye and deflected the ball between defender and goalkeeper. He hadn't scored for his country in three years (for two of those years he was banned) and he hadn't looked match fit in the first four games, but he ended up with a winner's medal, Top Scorer of the Tournament with six goals, and also Player of the Tournament. The bar was now turned up to 11! We were all dancing and singing and shouting at the ref to blow the whistle. Someone ordered grappa. Someone ordered some more.

Brazil only needed a draw to get through. They threw everything at the Italian wall of defenders but the Blues held firm. I now felt 99 per cent Italian with all the wine and the grappa. Then Italy scored again! It took us two full minutes to realise it had been ruled out as offside. With two minutes to go, the Brazilians had a free kick to the left. Eder whipped it in and Oscar met it fiercely at the back stick. Zoff dropped low to his left to save it brilliantly, but the ball was dribbling towards the line, where he stopped it. The Brazilian players were claiming it was over the line. The bar became loud with insults. Finally, the ref blew for full time. There was madness. We were all

quite drunk now, but more grappa was poured out –
the bar owner had given up charging anyone. I finally
left the bar, very drunk, at midnight and struggled
back up the hill to the campsite. I wondered what
would happen when my new friends returned to their
wives who had been on the candlelit parade while
they were watching the game.

I had a lot of trouble getting into my sleeping
bag that night and even more trouble climbing into
my hammock. I slept fitfully and awoke at sunrise,
still drunk.

11

The Pyrenees

I left Lourdes early, sneaking out of the campsite without paying as there was no one up to take my money. I was hungover from my night watching Italy v. Brazil in the World Cup with the Italian Catholics. I quickly caught a lift to Pau, where I treated myself to a croissant and a hot chocolate for breakfast. I wandered out of town to the A64, with the intention of getting to Bayonne, then across the border into Spain, and on to Pamplona for San Fermín, but after a bad day's hitching I had travelled only about 20 miles up the road to Orthez. It was a lot harder in France than in the UK to find friendly drivers. Of course, this might have had something to do with the activities of ETA, the Basque Separatists.

I decided to change my plans and go directly south over the Pyrenees to Jaca on the N34, and by 5pm I had reached Oloron-Sainte-Marie. I waited there for two hours, but there was hardly any traffic. In my rucksack I had my lightweight nylon hammock that I'd string between two trees at night when I needed to sleep rough. I'd throw a large piece of plastic over string tied above it, and once inside my sleeping bag I'd go to sleep in the hammock, safe from the elements. I was just looking around for a nearby wood when, out of the blue, a woman stopped in an open-top coupé.

She asked me where I was headed and I told her I was trying to get to Jaca. She waved me into the car and we were off. Her name was Eva and she explained that she worked in Bordeaux and was returning to her family home for her father's birthday. Then she suddenly suggested that I should come too. They had a spare room, there would be food and drink, and her father would be off to the local market in the morning and could drop me at the border. I couldn't believe my luck. I had to pinch myself!

Hitch-hiking could be like that. If I was waiting at one spot I would console myself with the thought that it was happening for a reason. This was proof. If I'd continued towards Bayonne, this lift wouldn't have happened. If I'd wandered off to find the woods five minutes earlier, I'd have missed this lift. This thinking would help me get through the day – and it's how I look at work, too. Being a self-employed comedian is a pretty hand-to-mouth existence, but I've never planned a career – it's just happened, by being optimistic and making the most of each opportunity that life throws up. Basically, I'm a hippy.

The car climbed and climbed into the mountains, until at last we turned off onto a dirt track. Half a mile later we pulled up outside a Basque farmhouse in the twilight. The ground floor was a garage and then there were three more floors above. Pyrenean farmhouses are huge, as all the family sticks together: when the son marries, he and his bride usually move in with their parents. The first floor was a large kitchen/dining room, with a big table surrounded by a very confused-looking family.

Eva introduced me to her parents first and I wished her father 'Bon Anniversaire'; then she introduced me to her brother and his wife, and to a brother and sister who were teenagers. Her mother showed me the state-of-the-art TV that the family had bought their father for his birthday. She explained that they'd purchased it three weeks earlier so that he could watch the World Cup. I told them that I'd been to Bilbao for the England v. France game on my birthday and there was a lot of tutting about the French performance that night. They were very impressed by my ticket stub, for some reason.

The unusual thing about the TV was that it was still in its box. One hole had been cut in the cardboard the same size as the screen and another over the control buttons. They saw me looking puzzled, and pointed up to the ceiling where there were about 20 legs of ham, hanging up to cure. Every so often one of them would drip blood or fat, so the box was to protect the TV from this. The top of the box was stained by three weeks of dripping. While we were eating later a drop fell into my red wine and I was told that it was considered lucky.

We had a feast that night – eight courses of Basque delicacies, and *beaucoup de vin* too. The youngest son fetched a guitar afterwards and sang Beatles songs, so I borrowed some oranges from the kitchen and did an impromptu juggling show for them. To reward this quite average display, the father brought out a bottle of the local pastis (which is like Pernod). Reader, we drank it. The whole blinking bottle. Just the two of us, watching the highlights of the matches played in Spain that week. We drank it with water and ice, and as it mixed with the wine I felt fantastic. I gushed my thanks to the family for sharing their celebration with me.

At about 11, everyone started going to bed. Eva told me that she had sorted everything out with her father and that he'd give me a lift if I helped him with some chores in the morning. The family then said their goodbyes as they were not going to be up that early in the morning. I thanked them all again for sharing such a great night. Then Eva showed me to what can only be described as a broom cupboard, but I couldn't have cared less, I was so drunk. I unrolled my sleeping bag and crashed.

The next thing I knew, someone was kicking me.

'Oi, oi!' I cried. Then, forcing my eyes open, I found myself staring up into the father's face. He wasn't the jovial patriarch of the previous evening. When I tried to move my head I realised why.

'*Quelle heure est-il, monsieur?*'

'*Cinq heures et demie,*' he growled back. He seemed to be enjoying my displeasure. This had to be some sort of joke. I tried to get up, which was a huge mistake – my head was as heavy as a Mini Cooper. I don't know if you have ever had a red wine and pastis hangover, but it's a level 9. There is only one worse: alcoholic poisoning, which is a category 10.

I've always taken pride in my hangovers; in fact, I try to enjoy them. After all, you've put the work in to create them. I have a top five hangovers: the worst ever was on 10 July 1985 (in Pamplona), followed by 1 January 1987 (Perth, Australia) – both of those were 10s. Then comes this one I'm about to describe, followed by 6 May 1979 (Liverpool) and 27 July 1993 (Glastonbury).

I could feel my brain peeling away from the inside of my skull. My mouth was as dry as a sandpit in the Sahara, every bone ached and my body was screaming at me to lie still. But a promise is a promise, and I needed that lift if I was going to make the opening ceremony in Pamplona. I forced myself to stand up and put some clothes on, but when I leaned forward to tie my shoelaces my head felt like it would fall off, so I left them untied. I headed down to the garage where Papa was waiting for me. He pointed to a cage with five lambs in it. Oh, I thought, we're going to have to lift that onto his truck. I couldn't have been more wrong.

He picked up the first lamb and brought it over to a work bench by the garage door. He then pulled out a pocket knife, opened it and slit the lamb's throat. He beckoned me over to the worktable and got me to hold the four legs so that the head was over the end and the blood could drain into a large bucket on the floor. The hangover was making me squeamish, and the poor little lamb kept trying to struggle out of my grasp, blood going all over my hands and forearms. The farmer wasn't happy when this occurred and he would snarl at me in Basque. Every so often I had to dry-heave. When the lamb finally stopped shaking I let it go and stood back from the table. Then I jumped out of my skin as the lamb tried to get to its feet. I grabbed it again and held on for another three minutes. As soon as my murderous friend realised it was dead, he slit the throat of the next lamb and handed it to me to repeat the process.

He then took the limp body of the first lamb and used the point of his knife to make a half-inch slit in the skin, by the ankle on one of the rear legs. I watched him fetch a foot pump from the wall and push the nozzle into the hole, under the skin, facing up the leg. He began to stamp on the foot pump with a regular beat. To my horror, as I stood holding one struggling creature, he started to make a lamb balloon out of its mate. The air was lifting the skin away from the carcass, up the back leg, down the other, then along the torso, down the front legs and along the neck. When it reached the eyes there was an explosion of air and, with a few quick cuts, the farmer removed the skin completely. As soon as the second lamb gave up the ghost, I ran out into the field and threw up.

By the fifth lamb, my stomach was raw from the retching, my mouth tasted of pastis and stomach acid, my eyes were watering and my head was pounding. I toyed with the idea of asking the farmer to do me next. He took the bucket of blood upstairs to the kitchen, then placed the dead lambs in a large Esky cooler and climbed into his truck. I ran and grabbed my bag and jumped in beside him. We headed off to the border as the sun rose over the mountains. They were stunning, but I couldn't enjoy them.

That was probably the worst morning's work I ever did. Before I started in this business we call show, I only actually had five proper jobs. None of them lasted more than six weeks. Firstly, there was the Saturday job at Wickes. I wasn't very good at it. I used to skive off in the cement bay, crawling under the shelves for a nap now and again. I had to help customers load their cars after they had made their purchases. It kept me fit, carrying bags of aggregate or porcelain toilets through the warehouse. Then there was Waitrose, which I've already covered.

The following summer I worked for a month as the night porter at the Queen's Hotel, Aldershot, by the polo fields. The manager was a big man called Tom Redhead. He was a friend of the family and that's how I got the job. Tom was also the team manager for the British Olympic shooting squad.

I loved that job. I have always been a night owl; I'm not a fan of mornings at all. I would cycle to the hotel at 10.30pm and take over reception. The bar would close at 11pm and then I would pretty much have the place to myself. My work consisted of manning the desk in order to greet any late arrivals and doing three security walks around the hotel at 1am, 3am and 5am. Then at 8am I would cycle home in the summer sunshine, smiling at those people in the morning traffic jams on their way to work. I watched the whole of Wimbledon that summer and had a great tan.

It wasn't exactly challenging work, although the hotel was rumoured to be haunted. When they had built the new wing in the 1960s they had filled in a small pond in the grounds of the hotel. According to local legend a seven-year-old girl had drowned in this pond during a birthday party in the 1920s. A few night porters had apparently seen a little girl walking the corridors of the new wing on all three floors. I don't believe in ghosts and maybe that's why I never witnessed her ethereal presence.

I had worked on a few wedding receptions at the hotel when they were short staffed that summer and knew the kitchen staff well. They would leave me a sandwich and any cream cakes that would have gone off by the next day. One night I had seven eclairs and two cream horns. I also worked out a way to get round the locks on the optics in the bar, and would have the odd brandy in my coffee throughout the night.

As Tom was the team manager, the Olympic shooting squad stayed the week at the hotel during the selection process at Bisley Shooting Grounds. This brought about another of my brushes with death.

One of the squad had taken a fancy to Sheila, a barmaid at the hotel. He sat on a stool at the bar all evening, drinking large whiskies. Sheila had been pleasant to him, but had batted back his clumsy chat-up lines with witty replies that were not meant to encourage him. He seemed to be a man of privilege – he had a tweed suit, a flash watch and he drove a Jag. He was obviously used to getting his own way, and the fact that Sheila wasn't interested in his advances was frustrating him immensely. After she closed up the bar, she passed by the desk and told me to keep my eye on him. As she was talking to me, he came up behind her and tried to grab her for a goodnight kiss, but she evaded his grasp and ran out the back door to the hotel.

'Where's she gone?' he slurred.

'Home I think, sir,' I replied, while inside I was screaming, 'Fuck off and leave her alone!'

'But she told me that she lived here at the hotel!'

'I wouldn't know, sir,' I muttered.

'Does she or does she not live here at the hotel?'

'I really don't know, sir, I only started last week,' I lied.

He was getting very red in the face. My polite replies were annoying him.

'Right!' he said a little too loudly, and marched off up the stairs to his room. I settled down to read my book, shaking my head at his rudeness.

But that wasn't the end of it. I think he must have had a bottle in his room, because I had just returned from my 1am patrol when he turned up, even more drunk, at my desk again. He was carrying a rifle. I don't know much about guns, but this looked like a heavy-duty weapon.

'The number?' he spat.

'Sorry,' I said. 'Which number do you require?' My mind was racing. Why had he brought a rifle to reception? Was it loaded? I realised I'd have to be very careful how I answered his questions. The counter was between the two of us and I would have to go through two doors to get round to the reception area.

'Her room number. The girl.' He was swaying alarmingly.

'Er, which girl?'

'The girl, the girl. You know!' he gestured to the bar.

'What was her name?' I asked innocently. This confused him. I don't think he had even thought to ask Sheila her name. His only thought was for his own pleasure, he didn't care about the feelings of anyone other than himself. As far as he was concerned it was his world and we just happened to live in it.

By answering his every question with a question I kept him talking for about 10 minutes before he remembered the gun he was holding. He slowly swung it round until it was pointing at my chest.

'Is that thing loaded?' I asked him nervously.

He stared at me for a couple of seconds, then nodded.

The pause suggested it wasn't. Or was he too drunk to remember? I consider myself a good poker player, but this was a different game altogether. My throat was dry, my palms were wet. I had to keep him sweet. I kept the conversation on a loop, hoping that he would fall asleep and I could grab the rifle. But he was a tough old bird, ex-army, and stubborn with it. My only thought, though, was that he must not get Sheila's room number. After about an hour I convinced him that we should ring Mr Redhead. I had explained that he was not only the shooting team manager but also the hotel manager, therefore he would know which rooms the staff stayed in. At first he hadn't wanted to involve Mr Redhead as it might look bad, but I had chivvied him into believing it was the only way he could get the room number.

I picked up the phone and rang the manager's flat on the top floor. Mr Redhead was furious at being woken up at three in the morning! He shouted down the line at me that my call had better be important.

'Um, yes, it is important,' I mumbled, staring at the barrel of the gun.

'Well, what's the matter, lad?'

'I have a guest here, at the desk. I believe he is a member of your shooting squad.' I told him the name of sex-starved guest.

'Well, what do you want me to do about it? Tell him to go to bed, he has a competition shoot in the morning,' he instructed me, angrily.

'He wants Sheila's room number. Sheila from the bar. He says they have a date... He is very insistent that I give it to him.' The guest was nodding along with this.

'Oh, and did I mention he is pointing a gun at me?' I said, smiling at the old duffer.

'Keep him talking. I'm on my way down!'

I replaced the receiver.

'What did he say?' he asked.

'He needs to come down to the office to find the staff book with the room numbers in.'

We stood in silence, with him swaying uncertainly and me staring at the barrel of the gun. Suddenly Tom Redhead came striding down the stairs three at a time. The gunman was suddenly subservient; Tom was an intimidating sight. I think the bloke realised that he was in charge of selection for the team, too. A pained look crossed his face and he lowered the gun till it pointed at the floor. Mr Redhead leapt forward and wrestled it from him. He then cuffed the guy round the back of the head and sent him to bed.

'I'll put this in the gun safe. He shouldn't have had it in his room. Carry on, Andrew.' Off he went, back to bed.

When I was sure neither of them were coming back, I crossed to the bar and poured myself a quadruple brandy. It was never mentioned again. But my next pay packet had an extra £20 note in it.

👍

In January of 1981, while I was living on the dole, my overdraft reached the magic figure of £100. I was called into see the bank manager, who told me that I would have to get some work as the bank would not extend my limit. At that time Liverpool had the highest unemployment rate in the country, so after signing off the dole, I hitched south to Mum and Dad's in Farnborough. On the Friday morning I headed to the Job Centre and found a job at the cosmetics company Lenthéric Morny Ltd, starting the following Monday. It paid £23 for the week.

I turned up bright and early at the factory in Camberley and was led to a conveyor belt with 20 other new workers. Our job was to take apart the Christmas gift sets and divide them up into their four separate constituents. I sat next to an Australian guy called Steve. He was a big Monty Python fan – that's why he had come to the UK. So, he and I sat all day doing Python sketches and roaring with laughter. Our fellow workers were, for the most part, middle-aged women and they were not impressed.

Our line was in charge of removing the soaps from the conveyor belt and stacking them into a new box, four at a time. The line started off quite slowly, but as the morning went on the speed increased. By lunchtime it was really travelling. We had been so immersed in our comedy workshop, we hadn't noticed some of the women removing the soaps from the Christmas boxes and stockpiling them. Just before the siren that signalled lunch, they shovelled these soaps onto the belt so that instead of coming past us at a rate of one per second, suddenly there were 30 every second – a wall of soap coming straight at us. We grabbed as many as we could but, as we were at the end of the line, most of them ended up on the floor. We missed the first 10 minutes of the lunch break as we picked them all up.

After four days all the Christmas boxes had been emptied, so Steve and I were moved to the hand-cream line. This was agony. At the start of the conveyor belt there was a machine that heat-sealed one end of the tube. The tubes were then dropped into a machine that filled them with thick white hand cream. Then the tubes were passed to another machine that affixed the neck end and they were dropped back onto the belt. Next, someone would partly screw a top on, before the next person on the line screwed the top tight and then it would come to us. We would pick it up and squeeze the middle of the tube to make sure that both ends were sealed properly. They came past at a rate of one per second.

This doesn't sound too hard, but you just try it now. A tube of toothpaste will suffice. Pick it up and squeeze it, then drop it, then repeat once every second. You'll soon notice that the repetitive action becomes painful very rapidly. I think it's the only time I have ever suffered from cramp in my thumb! Of course, if the tube was not sealed properly when squeezed, the contents would squirt out over whoever was standing next to you and the line would have to stop while we cleaned ourselves up. It was a double-edged sword: you looked like an extra in a porn-movie orgy, but you had some respite from squeezing tubes.

The worst day I spent at Lenthéric Morny was the one I spent working in the talc room. After we'd been taken upstairs and into a dressing room, the guy in charge told us to put on some white overalls, and then two white coats over our clothes. We were given paper hats and a gauze mask to place over our faces. Lastly, we were handed plastic goggles before being led into the talc room.

Talc is basically scented chalk dust. There were three machines that forced the talc into the plastic bottles at high speed before the top was moulded on. They would fill two dozen bottles and then drop them into a box. It was our job to carry the boxes out and load them onto a pallet before they were taken off to the loading bay.

Every time the machine squirted the talc into the bottle, finer grains of chalk would escape out the sides. Within half an hour of the machines starting up you couldn't see your hand in front of your face due to the amount of chalk in the air. You walked into the room through two doorways covered with thick plastic strips. Someone would bump into you and hand you a box and you would bring it out. At 10.30am there was a 15-minute coffee break. I had just entered the room at this point. The others thought it hilarious to leave for their breaks without telling me. I stood in the swirling chalk dust for five minutes and waited. Then I began shouting, but the noise from the machines made this a pointless exercise. I didn't want to move because I wasn't sure exactly where the machines were. In the end I spent the whole of my break standing in that white-out. That night I had three baths but I still couldn't get rid of all the talc, and then I went to the pub where my sweet smell turned a few heads.

Leaving me in the talc room was the last straw. I handed in my notice. On my last day I was put on a new line. Lenthéric were releasing a new perfume called *Panache*. My job was to take the tiny tester bottles from the conveyor belt and place them in presentation packaging. They were about an inch high and quarter of an inch wide. As the afternoon progressed I began putting them down my trousers into my underpants. I must have had about 20 of the little bottles down there: so many that I clinked when I walked. But I put my heavy overcoat on and left, knowing I would never be back. I had lasted two weeks and I had made a big enough dent in my overdraft. I also had birthday presents for the women in my life for the next two years.

The last proper job I had was in September 1982. I had yet again reached my £100 overdraft and hitched home to Farnborough to get enough money to pay it off. I visited the Job Centre and found a card on the stands for six weeks' work at Grants of St James's in Guildford. I applied and they took me on over the phone the next day.

They had a batch of white wine that had oxidised and needed to be decanted into vats to be sent back to France, where it would be turned into white wine vinegar. A total of 60,000 bottles in six weeks, or 2,000 bottles a day. There were six of us taken on to complete this task, all of us under 23. In charge was Bob, who had worked for the company for 47 years, man and boy. He had two months until his retirement. Consequently, he didn't mind how we filled the quota, just as long as we did. He spent the day reading *The Sun* (I caused quite a stir when I pulled out a *Guardian* in the canteen) and doing crosswords, occasionally doing a tally to see how many bottles we had shifted.

COMPANY GRANTS OF ST JAMES'S LTD	NAME OF DEDUCTION		CLOCK HOURS £
NAME SMART ANDREW KEITH			
CLOCK No. 2610183 P.A.C. 003	ERNI CAT. A	7.04	32.00
DEPT. 073 PAY FOR W/E 02/04/83			
	TAX	14.10	
TAX CODE 159L			
TAX WEEK 1 N.I. NO WE195189A			
GROSS PAY TO DATE 78.20			
TAX PAID TO DATE 14.10			
CO. PENSION TO DATE 0.00			
E.R.N.I. TO DATE 7.04	TOTAL DEDUCTIONS	21.14	

NOTES: 'R' against Tax denotes Tax Refund.
         NET PAY = Gross Pay less Total Deductions.
         Tax has been calculated after Company Pension has been deducted from Gross Pay.

There were two corkscrews attached to a heavy metal workbench: chunky great things that you inserted into the neck of the bottle, pulling the handle down then up again. You removed the bottle and placed it on the table, then pulled the handle down, removed the cork, then lifted the corkscrew again, ready for the next bottle. The fiddly bit was removing the cork, which had to be twisted off the corkscrew. Two lads did that while two others supplied the bottles from cardboard boxes containing 12 bottles each. The empty boxes were then placed on a pallet ready to receive the empty bottles. When there were 500 bottles on the pallet it would be taken to the loading bay. This was a journey of about 80 yards, through the storage area, then through the sherry-bottling plant, down a narrow thoroughfare between stacks of cases waiting to be sent to off-licences all over the country and then out onto the raised loading bay.

Once uncorked, the wine was poured into a large stainless-steel bath. From there it was sucked up by a pipe into a cylindrical vat on wheels that held 500 bottles. Once the pipe was detached, we found that if you put your nose over the aperture and sniffed as hard as you could, you would be drunk for about a minute and a half.

The first morning we were all over the place and after three hours we had done about 300 bottles. At the tea break, everyone was pretty down. I suggested we needed a system. We all chipped in with our ideas, then I suggested making it into a competition; three lads v three lads. The others were keen. We put in 50p each and gave it to Bob. The winners took the pot.

We couldn't wait to get back to work and soon the bottles were flying. We finished our 2,000 bottles at 4.45pm and spent the last 15 minutes sweeping up and tidying our area. I was on the losing team that day, but on the winning team about half the time in the days that followed. By the Friday of that first week we had it down to a fine art and finished by 4pm. The last hour we spent sitting on the cases of wine chatting about our weekend plans. One of the lads asked Bob if it was safe to drink the wine we were decanting.

'It depends,' he posited. 'If the bottle has been standing upright for a couple of hours the crystals should all be at the bottom of the bottle. I'm sure it would then be all right to drink the wine from the neck.' I have no way of knowing if this is true, but we did it anyway. We left that evening supporting each other to the clocking-off machine.

From then on, we were a happy band of brothers. We were never too drunk to work (well, not until we finished the 2,000 bottles anyway), but we were pretty merry. The weird thing was that at lunchtime we would go across the road and pay for a couple of pints and something to eat in the pub. Most days we would finish at four, but one Friday we really went for it sober. We finished at 3.15pm!

When competing in teams it quickly became apparent that when someone had to take the empty bottles to the loading bay on a hand-pulled forklift, the other team had an obvious advantage. So we set up another competition – who could do the fastest time from our little area out to the dock and back with the empty trolley. Everyone would stop uncorking and we would count down from five. Even empty, 500 bottles are quite heavy, so it took a good start to get them moving. But then the weight would kick in and cornering was a tricky business. As we flew through the sherry-bottling area, staffed solely by women, they would either cheer us on or shout insults.

Brian, who was the eldest and an ex-copper, set a very impressive time of two minutes and three seconds. I was determined to beat it. In fact, I wanted to be the first to break two minutes. When it came to my turn, I had worked out my start, determined the best line through each corner and stayed stone-cold sober. The boys counted down and I was off. It felt like a good run; I made the turn into Sherry Bottling perfectly. Coming out of Sherry into the narrow stretch between the crates of wine, I really went for it and made it through cleanly without touching the sides. I swung the handle to turn onto the loading bay, but I was going way too fast. Everything went into slow motion. The trolley was sliding on the smooth concrete and I realised there was nothing I could do stop its momentum. I threw myself clear and enjoyed the sound of 500 bottles flying through the air off the side of the loading bay and smashing on the tarmac. Apparently the whole factory heard it. All the lines were stopped. I lay on my back laughing. Ten minutes later I wasn't laughing – I was in the manager's office being hauled over the coals.

No one ever beat two minutes.

News of our productivity had reached higher up at the factory and with one week to go we were all rewarded with an offer of contracts for life at Grants of St James's. The other five lads were very excited. I was the only one who declined. The others seemed quite sad at my decision. My nickname was Smiler at the plant.

'Hey Smiler, what are you thinking of, mate?' said Brian.

'I don't want a nine-to-five job, Brian.'

'But what are you going to do? There are three million unemployed at the moment.'

'I'm going to be a juggler.' They all laughed.

'A fucking juggler!' grinned Brian. 'You're precious, Smiler!'

That night we went out to celebrate. We pub-crawled around Guildford, ending up in The Three Pigeons at the top of the High Street. I stumbled down the hill at 11, but I'd left it too late and I missed my last train back to Farnborough. I stood there drunkenly wondering what I should do. For some reason I headed toward the cathedral. Maybe I thought I'd be able to sleep on the pews, but on the way there I had to cross the university campus. I saw someone entering one of the halls of residence and followed them in. They went through the bottom corridor and I headed up the stairs. I'd had an idea. On the top floor I entered a corridor. It looked a lot like the layout we had in Liverpool: six rooms, a kitchen and two bathrooms. I went into one of the bathrooms and locked the door. I then climbed into the bath and fell fast asleep. I awoke at about 6am and left quietly, had breakfast in a cafe and turned up for work at 8.30. The boys ribbed me mercilessly for being in the same clothes as the day before.

I used the same trick the following Thursday, which was my leaving do. But that time I took a little travel alarm clock with me to make sure I didn't oversleep. I often wonder if those boys with their life contracts are still at Grants of St James's. They would be coming up for retirement about now. Blimey.

The French farmer dropped me at the border just past a ski resort called Candanchú, did a U-turn and headed back down the French side. The resort appeared to be closed for the summer – or maybe it was just too early – and there was nowhere to get a drink. In the distance I could see an army platoon repairing an avalanche fence. It was very quiet. Blissfully so! I was so busy watching the soldiers that I didn't see the car pulling up for me. The driver tooted the horn and I trudged across to the vehicle and threw my rucksack onto the back seat without asking where he was going. It was a young French guy in a suit heading to Zaragoza and he dropped me off at Jaca.

The junction was on the edge of a desert – nothing but sand with a road down the middle – and it was already 35°C at 8am. There was a heat haze shimmering over the tarmac. I have never been so thirsty in my life. I was there for two hours, with no shade. Finally, out of the shimmering heat came a jeep. I thought at first that the driver in a brown uniform might be a policeman, and I'd heard horror stories about how some Spanish local police forces treated hitch-hikers badly. I needn't have worried: it was a guy from the Spanish forestry commission. He was on his way to Pamplona and drove like a maniac to get us there before midday to see the rocket that announces the start of the fiesta.

12

Pamplona

The first thing you notice when you drive into Pamplona during the festival of San Fermín is that everyone is dressed the same. From babies aged one up to the 90-year-olds, everyone is wearing the same outfit: a white shirt, white trousers or skirt, a red sash around the waist and a red neckerchief – the national dress of the Basques. It is a magnificent sight. The town had a population of just over 140,000 in those days, but during the festival there were a million visitors over the week. The whole city spent the year looking forward to the start of this week in July. They have a song, which goes:

First of January,

Second of February,

Third of March,

Fourth of April,

Fifth of May,

Sixth of June,

Seventh of July, San Fermín.

To Pamplona we will go, with tights, with tights.

To Pamplona we will go, with a tight and a shock.

Catchy, huh?

However, the fiesta actually begins at midday on 6 July with an event called the *chupinazo*. A huge crowd gathers in front of the town hall where, at noon, a dignitary lets off a rocket from the first-floor balcony. As it explodes high above the town, the crowd goes crazy and the youths of the city throw champagne, flour, ketchup and eggs over each other. The festival has begun. I had arrived in town at 11.30 and, not knowing the form, I had made my way to the large town square. It, too, was full. The people here were older than those in front of the town hall, but they still cheered and threw their drinks in the air as the rocket burst. I bumped into two Americans, John and Linda, who were Interrailing. It was their first time, too. We decided to get rid of our bags and John, who spoke some Spanish, found out that there was a left-luggage office at the bus station.

When we arrived we found a sign written on a piece of cardboard that said 'Full'. There were crowds everywhere. Linda and I sat on our bags while John stopped people in the street and asked them what we could do with our luggage. A middle-aged guy stopped with his family; he asked John how many bags we had and then got us to follow him. He took us to an office where he worked on Avenida de Yanguas y Miranda and said we could leave our bags there. We could meet him at 9.30 the next morning to get them back. We thanked him profusely and headed back into town.

I was determined to check out the route of the bull run and obtained a map from the information point at the bus station. I asked the young Basque girl to mark the run on it, and off we went. We did the run in reverse, starting at the bullring. Outside the ring, in front of the box office, were stalls selling all the gear you needed to fit in. I bought a white T-shirt, a red scarf and a sash and immediately put them on. Next to the end stall was the fence for the run downhill to the ring. The course there was 15 feet across and sloped down to two huge red iron doors. The fence was made of enormous blocks of wood between posts that went into the cobbles. The run didn't look that wide and I thought I might be able to jump out if there was trouble, or I could dive and roll underneath the fence. Oh, how naive I was then.

We made our way from the bullring down Calle Estafeta. The crowds were filling the bars now and you could feel the excitement in the air. When we got to Calle Mercaderes, we turned off the route of the run in search of something to drink. I had gulped down a litre of lemonade when I arrived but still had a pastis hangover to quell. The bars weren't that expensive but we found a shop where they sold cheap bottles of ice-cold sangria, which tasted like fruit juice. That was when we heard the cheer. We went to see what was happening.

There was a square (more of a triangle really) with a pillar-like monument at its centre, dedicated to St Cecilia, its base surrounded by water fountains. There were three bars around the square, the most famous of which was the Mussel Bar – English-speaking visitors all knew the square by the name of the bar. Gathered around the base of the central pillar was a throng of Australians, Americans, British, Swedes, Germans and a few locals. They were all drunk, without exception! Most of them were wearing wine-stained shirts and trousers and some of the women just had bikini tops on. Every so often someone would climb the pillar – which wasn't easy as there was an overhang at the top. Their mates would push and shove them, standing on the drinking fountains to do so. Once they reached the top, which was a large concrete ball, a cheer would go up. Their friends and anyone else who wanted to join in would form two lines facing each other below them and then they would reach across to each other, grabbing tight hold of their hands. This created a cradle for the person on top of the pillar to dive into. It involved a lot of trust in the catchers. The trick was to throw yourself straight out from the monument so you landed flat on as many catchers' arms as possible. I did it twice, once in 1984 and again in 1988. It was frightening! The top section was cut off the monument in the early 2000s after some bad landings and broken legs and collar bones.

The afternoon passed in a blur. Wherever I turned, someone would offer me a wine skin to drink from, although about half the wine ended up on my shirt. By early evening I looked the same as everyone else in the square. John, Linda and I took a walk past the cathedral and to the town walls, where the view towards the Pyrenees was stunning. We had a nap under a tree for a couple of hours before heading back into the mêlée. The whole town seemed drunk. Everyone was dancing and, after the evening's bullfight, bands appeared, representing the different areas of the town.

Each band was made up of 20 to 30 people playing reedy local pipes (like wailing clarinets), drums, trumpets, trombones and French horns. They would slowly wend their way through the narrow streets of the old town, stopping outside certain bars where trays of beer and wine would be brought out for the players. We followed one of these for a while and ended up by the Hotel Tres Reyes.

I realised that we were not far from the bus station, where earlier we had noticed a funfair on the grass opposite, next to the castle. It was huge and had all the usual rides – dodgems, waltzers, carousels, helter-skelters and even a small roller coaster. In between there were restaurant tents serving marvellous paella and rotisserie chicken. I found a store selling sherry served in a large shot glass with a wafer-biscuit straw that you drank it through – we had a couple of those – and then we decided to go on the big wheel. There was quite a queue, but it was worth it: the view from the top was amazing, with the walls of the castle lit up by the fairground lights. We noticed a large crowd gathering in front of the bus station, covering the dual carriageway and the central reservation too, so after our ride we went to find out what they were doing. Although it was now 10 o'clock, whole families were gathered there, the little three-year-old kids so cute in their Basque outfits. There was a massive bang and we found out why they were there. The firework display!

Every night during the week of San Fermín there is a fantastic firework display that lasts 20 minutes. I have been all round the world in my time and have seen many displays, but none compare with the show you get in Pamplona. After 10 minutes you're exhausted. The end fills the sky with sparkles and leaves you shaking with its enormity. Someone told me that each display is voted on in a competition run by the local paper, and the company supplying the fireworks for the display that gets the most marks goes on to win a lot of big contracts for other fiestas throughout Spain.

After the fireworks we made our way back into the town, heading for the main square, Plaza del Castillo. We found ourselves in the mayhem that is the Calle San Gregorio, a long straight street where every other building seemed to be a bar. Loud music – sometimes pop songs, sometimes traditional Basque dance tunes – burst from every door, luring you in. I was so drunk by this point I was bouncing off the walls, trying to join in with the dancers. Although everyone was drinking a lot, there were no fights. Everyone was happy.

If you wanted to move down the street, you had to push through the crowd – but then we met a band coming the other way. The bands had picked up a hundred or so followers by this time, and family, friends and people who just wanted to dance were bearing down on us. There was only one thing to do: duck into another bar. This one was narrow and dark. We ordered three beers and watched the band pass by outside. A guy at the bar bought a litre of beer in a plastic glass and the barman handed him a toothpick, which he used to make three holes in the base of the container. He then held it high in front of him, and as the beer began to fly out in an arc, his friends rushed in with open mouths to drink.

When one person couldn't drink any more, another would take their place. The whole lot was gone in three minutes.

After the band had gone, we carried on down the street, eventually coming out in the large open space that is the main square. Around the edge of the square there were small trees, flower beds and a well-kept lawn. This was covered in people asleep or just lying down drinking and smoking. I found out that this was where up to 2,000 people would spend the night, since hotels charge a premium rate during the festival. In the centre of this space was a large circular bandstand, its stage about 10 feet off the ground, and on this stage was a local heavy-metal band. We dived into the middle of the pogoing crowd, where somehow I lost John and Linda. I think maybe they lost me on purpose after seeing my dancing. I don't remember much after that. I know my plan was to do the bull run the next morning, but that's all I had.

👍

I woke up on a landing with my back against a cast-iron balustrade. I was fully clothed and suffering with my second major hangover in two days. Looking back, with the dehydration from standing in the desert the day before, and then all the alcohol and not eating all day because my stomach was full of sangria, I think it was probably alcoholic poisoning. I struggled to sit up. It was hard. My clothes were stained red from the wine. And then I noticed that my wallet had gone – and my passport. There were cheers in the distance, which I realised were for the bull run. I had missed it.

My addled brain tried to decipher what all this meant. I went downstairs two floors to the street, and attempted to work out what had happened. I must have seen someone going into the house, which was made up of eight flats, and followed them in, thinking that I could sleep on the staircase. Then, during the night, someone must have found me in a comatose state and taken everything.

I found I was on the street between Calle Mercaderes, which the bull run passed through, and the Mussel Bar. People were streaming away from the run towards me and I let myself be borne along with the crowd to St Cecilia's fountain. I found a plastic glass that hadn't been crushed underfoot, filled it from the drinking fountain and gulped the water down greedily. I needed a plan.

I stumbled round the back streets, my head a block of concrete, my tongue a wedge of Jarlsberg. Then I remembered that my rucksack had to be collected at 9.30. I somehow managed to navigate through the crowds emptying from the bullring after the *encierro* and found myself back opposite the funfair, looking for the office door. Luckily, I bumped into John and Linda;

they had slept in the main square and had watched the run from a side street, but they complained that they hadn't seen anything as it had shot past them in a few seconds. I explained what I thought had happened to me. They gave me some chocolate milk and asked me what I was going to do. At this juncture the guy who owned the office turned up and John explained my plight in broken Spanish.

He was brilliant. He told us that the nearest British embassy was in Bilbao and suggested that I go to the police station first and report the theft. Then he very generously gave me £5 in pesetas to cover my food and drink and the bus fare. (I went back three years later, paid him back and gave him a nice bottle of cognac for his kindness.) John volunteered to come with me to the police station to translate, but when we arrived there was an English-speaking cop just inside the door. The festival crowds attract Europe's top pickpockets – something it's worth bearing in mind when you're there. I was one of 12 people waiting to be seen and we all swapped stories of how we'd been robbed. My story was the least impressive. There were Australians and Americans who all seemed to be going to Madrid, as their embassies were there.

Eventually I was seen. They took down my report and I was given a copy to give to the embassy. The policeman said I should go straight to the bus station and head to Bilbao as I was now undocumented, but I still wanted to do the bull run. I left the police station and went to buy a bus ticket; there was a bus the following morning at 10. I changed out of my wine-soaked T-shirt, but the only clean top I had was a bright yellow vest with the logo 'Remember You're A Womble'. Next, I managed to put my rucksack into a left-luggage locker, which left me with about 50p. I was so dehydrated that I spent my remaining money on two bottles of water and headed back to the main square, where I sat on a bench wondering what to do. I needed to get some more money. An American woman sat down next to me. She had just been to the fresh produce market in the big hall just off the bull run and she offered me an orange after hearing my story. I had an idea and asked for her help.

'This is going to sound weird, and a little bit cheeky, but could you possibly let me have all four of those oranges? I think I might be able to make some money with them,' I asked politely.

'Of course,' she replied.

I took the brown paper bag from her and began to juggle with the oranges. At first I just worked through different patterns that I could do and finished with four oranges at once. All that practice I had done on the beach paid off – even in my hungover state I rarely dropped an orange. Anyway, they were too valuable to be dropped, as they might split. I soon had a small crowd of people who had been crossing the square. At the end I put down my San Fermín scarf and a few people came forward and put some coppers on it. I was off.

It was a blisteringly hot day again, not a breath of wind. I needed some shade. The north end of the plaza was dominated by the grand Hotel Iruña, which was still a hotel in those days. In fact, just 25 years earlier, Hemingway had stayed there when he was in town, together with the matadors who he would write about. The downstairs was one massive bar; tragically, it's now only a bar during the festival, and the rest of the year it's a bingo hall. It is an amazing building and in those days was the hub of the fiesta.

All the buildings in the square have a covered walkway built onto their fronts, and it was into this covered area that I took my act. Each time I did my little show I would try to add a bit. A bump off my elbow or knee, or a new pattern. If I heard English voices I would hail them and then make jokes about where they were from or if they had done the bull run. This worked even better than the juggling and my takings went up.

As the sun went down below the buildings, I took myself off to the bullring as the crowd for that night's bullfight was gathering. I juggled for them until they had all gone into the ring and then I went to get something to eat. I crossed the road and entered La Olla – still my favourite restaurant in the town. It's where you'll find me after a run, drinking strong black coffee and a large brandy. You haven't lived till you have eaten their one-kilo steak cooked on the bone – it takes three people to eat one! They had *pinchos* (the Basque for tapas, usually seafood or Bayonne ham) on the bar and I tucked into a few of these and had a glass of beer. I counted up my money and found I had made about £20.

From there I headed back to the main square, as there are numerous restaurants, bars and cafes around its edge, with tables and chairs and umbrellas to keep off the sun. Here was a captive audience. I would ask the people at the tables nearest the middle of the square if they wanted a quick juggling show and, if they did, I would start. At the end some gave me money and some gave me beer or food.

Some lads from Sunderland looked after me royally; when I rose from my seat to leave their table, one of them who had listened to my sorry tale gave me a £10 note that I tucked into my sock for safekeeping. By now I had made nearly £50 and so I decided to stop work for the day. It had been wonderful. I thought of the jobs I had done in Grants of St James's and Lenthéric Morny where I had worked eight-hour shifts for £2 an hour; this seemed a much better way to make a living. There must be places in the UK where I could do this, I thought. And that was that. I had finally found a way to get paid for entertaining. I could choose when I worked – it was perfect. But I still had to get home!

Also, it was now only nine hours till the bull run. I decided to head to the bus station to watch the fireworks. I bought a bottle of sangria for about 30p and strolled through the crowded streets. The fireworks were amazing again and I fell in with some Aussies who had just arrived. I led them through the street to their hostel and then we all headed to the Mussel Bar, as this seemed to be where the English-speaking runners hung out. I had stopped drinking at this point, as I wanted a clear head for the morning and didn't want a repeat of the night before. We met a guy from Melbourne who had done the run that morning and who said he would show us what to do. He took us back to Calle Mercaderes and down to the town hall (it was the first time I saw this magnificent structure). He explained that you had to climb through the two safety fences into the run at this point and wait till 7.55am; the police would then let you walk to where you wanted to start from. He said he had started at the bottom of Estafeta and the bulls had passed him in front of the Telefónica building, the widest part of the course. We followed the run down the hill to the right of the town hall and past the side street that led to the market. Then, after passing two sets of steps into a canyon between a solid rock wall on one side and a new rectangular building on the other, we reached the holding pen. The bulls are brought there at 3am, just five hours before the run.

I said goodbye to the Aussies and began walking round the old town. I find that it's easier to stay awake if I'm walking – just ambling along watching everyone, drifting like a ghost through their revelries.

At about 2.30am I found myself back at the holding pen, so I took a seat high on the wall of the old town's fortifications to watch the bulls arrive. These animals are not like anything you would see on a British farm; they have been bred for thousands of years from the fighting bulls of the Camargue region. They are killing machines – territorial, muscular, powerful killers. Once they were in the pen I walked down to the viewing platform. They looked huge (the average weight of a fighting bull is half a ton). Some of them were lying down, and there were six even bigger steers in the pen with them, which were to keep the bulls running together in a group.

After I'd spent 20 minutes staring at these magnificent beasts, I headed back up the run. In those days there used to be a scaffolding tower, about 20 feet high, at the junction of Mercaderes and Estafeta. This is the maddest part of the run, as the bulls pick up speed travelling down Mercaderes before reaching this 90-degree bend. Nowadays they spray the cobbled streets with an anti-slip covering, but back then the cobbles were usually wet from being hosed clean of broken glass and plastic cups. There was also a six-inch kerb along either side of the run about three feet from the wall. There would always be a pile-up on this corner and woe betide any runner caught up in it! I climbed the tower easily and sat waving to the passers-by until the TV crew turned up at 6.30.

It was time for my first run. I have completed 61 runs to date and surprisingly that first one was the easiest – but that was because I didn't know what to expect. I had no concept of the danger I would be in and I had no idea where that danger would come from. But as I climbed down from my perch, my heart was already racing and my mouth was dry.

13

Calle Estafeta

I made my way to the square in front of the town hall. It was already filling up with runners, watched by the drinkers who hadn't quite made it home the night before. It was 6.55am. During the night, local town-council workers had erected two rows of safety fences in the gaps between the houses. The run here is a slow left-handed curve through the square, and a lot of the oldies who do the run hug the inside fence of the curve because the bulls tend to go wide at this point. Before the run, this is where you wait. It is one of the scariest places on the planet as far as I'm concerned, but it's what happens to your brain that is scary.

My throat was already dry. The size and weight of the fence posts remind you that you are running with mighty beasts. People don't like making eye contact, because if they do you can see the fear – and you know you probably look the same to them. People talk in whispers, their voices broken by the time of day and the dryness of their mouths. There is a large, ornate clock at the top of the town hall and you look up at it every 20 seconds, wondering why it hasn't moved, wondering if it is broken. Time ceases to obey its normal rules. Adrenaline is released by your body, slowly at first, increasing your heart rate.

I thought about jumping through the fence and running down to watch in the bullring – I still had plenty of time. Then a policeman was pushing me through the first fence against my protestations. Everyone else was being thrown out too. I couldn't understand what was going on, but at 7.15 it all became clear. A rocket burst above the square and I watched in amazement as small children began running past, some as young as five. They were with their dads and they were all running along, looking back over their shoulders. Suddenly a cheer went up and half a dozen six-month-old bulls came hurtling down the centre of the street. This was the children's bull run for 6–13-year-olds; it started at the market, behind the town hall, and went all the way to the ring. It's amazing to think that this continued into the late 1980s.

Once they had passed by, we were allowed back into the run from between the two safety fences. It was back to the waiting. I noticed that a lot of runners were holding rolled-up newspapers. I later learned why. Bulls are colour-blind, so it's a myth that they go for red. And they have particularly bad eyesight, so they look for movement – that's why they charge the cape in a bullfight. Each runner waves the newspaper on their strong side, the side on which they want the bull to pass them, and the bull will supposedly follow the newspaper and not the man. The bulls run with six massive steers who keep them moving, and it's very important that you count them as they pass you. It's not always easy in the mayhem, but it's good to know if there is a loose one bringing up the rear. After the run has been going for two minutes, three more steers are released into the run to pick up any bulls who have become separated from the rest. The tourists' reactions to these three huge animals bearing down on them always make the Spanish crowd laugh. One year I was in Mercaderes after the bulls had passed me in the town-hall square. I waited for the clean-up steers to arrive and then stood perfectly still in their path. Luckily, at the last second they stepped round me, but I wouldn't do it again.

I headed down the hill in search of a newspaper. *Navarra Hoy* had just begun publication that year and I purchased one. I sat down and leafed through it. Not a good idea. There were lots of pictures of people getting hit by bulls on the day before's run, but the page that really grabbed my attention was towards the back. There were pictures of each of the six bulls with their names and weights underneath. That morning the bulls were from the Miura ranch; they come from a different ranch each day – always the best in Spain – and it's considered a great honour to supply the bulls for the fiesta. Each ranch's bulls have their own characteristics; in all the runs I've done, the bad ones have always been against Miura's bulls, which have wide horns and big chests and run very fast.

Feeling very nervous, I made my way back to the square. Nothing much had changed. A couple of lads from Barcelona, judging from their football shirts, were drinking a dark red wine straight from the bottle. I became fascinated by the cobblestones, which had been freshly washed. Two hours before, they had been covered in broken glass and plastic glasses, cigarette ends and food wrappers, but now the dark browny-blue cobbles glistened in the morning sun. Then someone pointed up at the sky and we all looked up to see a hot-air balloon drifting over the town. I just wanted the run to start. I looked up at the clock and it said 7.45. It felt like a year had passed since I bought my newspaper.

I started chatting to two Americans standing next to me who had run the day before. We talked about their experiences and then they told me about the statue. Before each *encierro*, as the run is called, the runners head down the hill, nearer to the holding pen. At 7.50am a foot-high statue of San Fermín is placed in a small niche in the right-hand wall of the

course, about 10 feet above the road. Newspapers held above their heads, the runners chant a song asking for the saint to look after them during the run. It translates as: 'We ask San Fermín to be our patron saint and to guide us in the running of the bulls, giving us his blessing.' This is sung three times, but as it was my first run I left after one verse and headed back to the town hall. Those last nine minutes were the worst – time really did stand still. I checked the faces of those around me; they were ashen. People were jogging from one foot to the other, while those who knew what they were doing were busy stretching. At the top of the square there was a line of policemen, arms linked, blocking us in. A few latecomers were still climbing through the fence – some straight from their beds by the look of their hair.

Then, at 7.55, the police stepped out of the way and we were allowed to walk the bull run to our starting points. I didn't have a clue where the best spot would be, but I walked along Mercaderes to the right-angled bend onto Estafeta (this bend has since been nicknamed Dead Man's Curve by the regular English-speaking runners). I just wanted to get away from that damn clock on the town hall. As it turned out, it wasn't a bad place to start the run.

The course is 825 metres long, or just over half a mile, and the bulls can cover it in two minutes 20 seconds on a good run. But then, everyone gets out of their way. For the human runners, life isn't so easy. The streets that the course follows are about 30 feet wide for the most part and there were about 1,800 people in the run that morning, so it gets very crowded. No one knows how the bull run started, but there are records from 1787 saying that it was well established then.

By now I was jumping up and down on the spot. I could almost taste the adrenaline. Either side of the run there are five-storey buildings. The ground floor is usually a shop, bar or restaurant, and these have large wooden boards placed over them. The upper floors are residential flats and each window has a balcony. As I looked down the street towards the bullring, it took a few seconds to take in the sight. Every balcony had at least five people standing on it and they were all in their fiesta costumes. It looked like a rocky canyon covered in red and white flowers. Was I really going to do this? I looked at the safety fence. There were so many people crushed against it that there was no way out. Of course, during the run they will let you out, but not if you attempt to climb over the top. I tried it once and I received a rap on the knuckles from a policeman's baton. Their reasoning is that you might bring down other runners who are looking back over their shoulders while you're climbing the fence. So you have to throw yourself onto the ground and roll under the bottom bar of the fence.

A rocket burst in the air above us and my heart missed a beat. Everything around me seemed to be going fast while I appeared to be moving very slowly in the centre of this chaos. The first rocket means they have swung open the massive gate on the holding pen. As we all took our first steps, we waited for the second rocket to tell us that all the bulls had left the pen. After about 30 yards we heard it. Good! That meant the bulls were running together – the last thing you want is a long gap. If a bull becomes separated from the others, that's when the run is at its most dangerous.

My plan was to jog at the start and see what was happening, but the adrenaline had other ideas. My legs were off. I tried to talk to them: 'Slow down, slow down.'

But there were others around me now and we kept a steady pace. Some people were hugging the wall, watching the balconies back at the corner. As the bulls are shorter than the runners, you can't see them if you look back down the street and so you have to take your cue from the people watching on the balconies. These wall-huggers are a nuisance and it is best to run about four feet out from the wall. Other people stand in the middle of the street and you have to body swerve around them as you snap your head forwards. To keep your balance, you have to run with your hand between the shoulder blades of the guy in front of you and hope that he doesn't go down.

If you do fall over, you must cover your head and lie still and then – hopefully – the bulls will jump over you. I have done this a few times over the years. You feel like your heart has stopped beating for five seconds as six bulls and six steers leap over your prone body. The worst thing is the noise you hear through the cobblestones as they rumble over you. And then suddenly hands are reaching out to you and dragging you to the side of the road.

About 50 seconds into the run I reached the crossroads of Calles Javier and Estafeta. Calle Javier is not much more than an alleyway – never watch the run from here, as you'll only see about one and a half seconds of the *encierro*. I was breathing heavily now and it felt like I was in a large tumble dryer with loads of strangers. Sometimes I would feel a hand on my back and sometimes I'd have to hurdle a fallen runner. It was like a big game of British bulldog, and still the bulls had not caught up with us. You have to have quick feet and an even quicker mind to adapt to the constantly changing movements of those around you. In the 1990s I once looked up and found myself running alongside Jean Condom, the French rugby-union international, and he had no trouble weaving through the crowd.

After Travesía Espoz y Mina, a lane that comes in from the right, the road becomes slightly wider. I looked back and could see from the spectators on the balconies that the bulls were about 50 yards behind me. I didn't think I could run any faster but I did, and as I reached the Telefónica building the first bull appeared by my right hip. One second they were nowhere to be seen; the next the crowd parted and there they were. They were beautiful. All six were as black as night. I waved my newspaper to my side, in front of the nose of the second bull. For the first time I had some room, as everyone was throwing themselves to the side of the run. I lasted about 30 yards before my legs gave out and I dived onto the road and rolled towards the fence. I saw more bulls go by in a blur, away down the slope into the Plaza de Toros, although I wasn't sure how many passed me. People helped me up and I started to run towards the stadium, chasing after them. I ran down the slope between the safety fences and into the tunnel under the stands. After the bright morning sunlight it was suddenly very dark in the tunnel, and then I was out in the ring – the third largest in the world and full of colour. A rocket went off and 25,000 people cheered. I'd survived.

The sky above looked so blue. I gasped down air, trying to fill my screaming lungs. Where every face before the run had been ashen white and serious, now they were flushed with joy and everyone was laughing as they were reunited with friends. I walked to the middle of the ring and turned slowly through 360 degrees. What a sight! I was hooked.

I thought that was the end of the *encierro*, but I was wrong. The door we had just come through was closed behind us, along with the safety-fence gates. But everyone's focus seemed to be on the opposite side of the ring. A few people were sitting cross-legged in front of a door, and there, on a small plinth above it, was a very bored-looking chief of police. The crowd chanted for him to give the signal to open the door and eventually he nodded to a small man standing between the safety fence and the wall of the ring. He grabbed the iron door and pulled it open to reveal a smaller tunnel. I was now about 20 yards away, peering into the darkness. A small bull, a year and a half old, shot out of the entrance and ran straight towards me, leaping over the seated nutters in front of the door. It was like a whirlwind. Around its horns was a leather covering to prevent it goring anyone, but it was still causing a lot of damage to those not quick enough to get out of the way. The crowd in the stands was loving watching the tourists being tossed in the air.

Then an Aussie grabbed the bull's tail. The crowd whistled and booed and Spaniards ran into the ring, punching him until he released his grip. You are not allowed to grab the bulls anywhere, as it is considered disrespectful. You are not even allowed to hit them with your rolled-up newspaper. This must seem strange, I know, but fighting bulls are respected throughout Spain.

After a few minutes the calf became slower, and before it tired itself out the chief of police signalled for it to be taken out. This is done by letting a huge ox into the ring; it jogs around slowly, collects the young bull, and then the pair are run out together. The chanting began again and soon the second bull was in the ring. Using my newspaper as a mini cape, I tried to attract its attention, but the crowd was swirling around it and it was charging randomly.

By the time the third bull was released I had become a bit cocky. I had survived the bull run and two smaller bulls and for some insane reason I decided to walk 10 yards from the safety fence and stand on my head, pushing my feet straight up. It must have looked quite strange, this lanky Englishman in a yellow 'Remember You're A Womble' vest and cut-off denim shorts, upside down on the sand.

Knowing what I know now, I would never have done this. Youth, adrenaline and overconfidence made me do it. I was working on the theory that if I stayed perfectly still the bull wouldn't go for me. Somehow this came off. When I jumped to my feet, the crowd on that side of the stadium gave me a big cheer. Bloody stupid!

A couple of years later, in 1984, I returned to Pamplona with Angelo Abela, my partner in The Vicious Boys. I took him through his first run and afterwards we were in the ring for the young bulls. That morning a particularly nasty police chief let a second young bull into the ring before the first had gone out. I was watching the first bull chase after Angelo, laughing my head off, when someone called my name; as I turned round I was hit by the second bull. Luckily, the horns went either side of me, but it hit me with such force that I was lifted clean out of my canvas shoes and the impact knocked all the air out of my body. I found myself lying along the bull's back with a leg over each eye so it couldn't see. I was wearing shorts and could feel its snot on my bare thighs. I was now travelling backwards at about 30 miles an hour. It is very unnerving to hear a sharp intake of breath from 25,000 people all at once.

I realised that the safety fence was coming up fast behind me and that I had to get off, and I really didn't want to slide down under the hooves. When I lifted my right leg to throw myself down the bull's left flank, it must have seen the upcoming fence. It planted its front feet in the sand and tossed me high in the air. I landed by the safety fence in a heap, lying there winded as people to the side tried to get the bull away from me by waving their newspapers.

Two Kiwis jumped over the fence, one grabbed my shoulders and the other my knees, and they threw me over the barrier. I landed on my left side on the concrete. I was in agony as the ridge between the bull's horns had fractured two ribs. Medical people came running and within minutes I was in an ambulance on the way to the hospital. After a couple of X-rays, they gave me some strong painkillers and sent me back out into the fiesta. The city of Pamplona pays all the medical bills of anyone hurt in the run as they know that no insurance company in their right mind would pay out.

After the last bull has left the ring (you know when that is because the police chief leaves his seat), the arena doors are opened to allow those in the ring to re-enter the party outside on the street. After that first run, I made my way to La Olla, ordered a half of lager and joined in the animated conversations of others who had participated in the morning's excitement. They were showing a rerun of the bull run on the TV in the next bar and we ran round to watch, hoping to see ourselves on the screen. I caught a glimpse of myself looking very scared. Time was getting on, though, and I needed to head to the bus station to catch the bus to Bilbao. I was going home.

14

Back to Farnborough

The bus was crowded with people leaving town after the bull run, but I managed to sit in a window seat. I was full of adrenaline despite the fact I had slept for only about 12 hours in the previous four days, but as soon as my head touched the window I fell fast asleep. I woke briefly in San Sebastián, then slept right through to the bus station in Bilbao. We decanted from the bus and I fetched my rucksack from the luggage hold. I found the information desk, and I asked the people there to mark on a map where the British Embassy was. It was another warm day and I arrived covered in sweat and looking like I had been away from home for years, but now I was going to get help from my government and soon I would be back in Blighty.

I was shown into a waiting room where there were already quite a few people. England had limped out of the World Cup; they'd had a very lame 0–0 draw against Germany and then, three days before I arrived in Bilbao, another 0–0 draw with Spain in the second group stage. Some of the England hooligans had made Bilbao their home for the tournament, as the first three games had been played there, so after England's departure they had returned from Madrid and had smashed up some bars in the old town. After two days in the cells, they were now being deported back home. The staff at the embassy managed to look both disgusted and scared by this mob in their waiting room, and at first they thought I was part of the gang. Eventually I managed to explain my problem to a young guy in a very nice grey suit. He fast-tracked me into a small office and listened intently to my story.

'So what can I do now? Can you get me home?' I asked plaintively.

'Well, we can give you a 48-hour temporary passport. That should give you enough time to get home.'

Then he told me that I'd have to pay for this temporary passport. I was about 50p short. He asked for my bank details, but I pointed out that I had emptied my bank account before my journey – I had even maxed out my overdraft limit. I asked if the embassy could lend me the money and I would send them a cheque when I arrived home. I thought that if they lent me enough I'd be able to get the ferry back from Santander. He explained that the embassy wasn't a bank and they couldn't even lend me 50p! I realised with dread that I wouldn't be getting a train or boat home; I was going to have to hitch 1,000 miles in 48 hours. It made the time I hitched from Liverpool to Ben Nevis and back for a bet seem like a breeze.

I went into the room where the football hooligans were sitting. They seemed happy to have a distraction to break their long wait and so I told them about how I had been robbed and how I had wanted to do the bull run, so had stayed for an extra day. I told them all about the run, too. When I'd finished a lad from Bolton fished a few pesetas from his jeans pocket. I could have hugged him, though I'm glad I didn't!

I returned to the small office and handed the money to the diplomat. He took my photo against a white wall and made up a temporary passport. It was now 5pm. I thanked him for his help and headed out into the evening rush hour. I walked a couple of miles to the N634 and stuck out my thumb. After an hour I managed to get a lift from a young lad in a flash car who took me to San Sebastián, but I then had to walk across the city to the next junction. I was there till nearly midnight waiting for a lift – it was worth the wait, though, as a German lorry driver stopped and said he would take me to Montpellier. This was great.

I had intended to head up the west coast of France, but this meant I was going across country, from where I could hopefully pick up a lift to Paris. My mantra in those days was 'take the lift you are offered'. Anyway, I had been waiting for four hours and I wasn't going to turn him down.

He didn't speak English and I didn't speak any German as I'd been thrown out of German classes after one term. (A footnote to this is that our German teacher at Farnborough Grammar School had been Mr Cutts. He came from Cologne and insisted on us calling him Herr Cutts. Oh, how we laughed! Every time.) So the driver and I just stared ahead into the night, watching the white lines rush beneath us. The occasional house was lit up in the foothills of the Pyrenees and I tried to imagine what people were doing in those houses, making up stories about the occupants — I still do that on long car journeys. We reached Montpellier at about 4am. I must have dozed off because my new German friend had to shake me to let me know we had arrived. I thanked him with a 'Danke schön!' and climbed down from the cab.

Within five minutes I was in another lorry cab, this one driven by a Spaniard. I proudly showed him my Pamplona scarf and mimed running with the bulls. He placed his forefinger next to his temple and rotated it before exclaiming, 'Loco!' He was headed to Avignon. We talked in French about the poor efforts of our national football teams at the World Cup. He was very sad that Spain wouldn't be playing in the final, but we both thought Italy should win.

As I climbed down from the cab, the sun was just breaking over the horizon – see, I still remember the word. I found myself at the start of a long straight bit of road cutting between two pine forests. There wasn't much traffic – about one vehicle every five minutes. I saw a brown Mercedes speeding toward me and put out my thumb half-heartedly, as I thought there was no way it would be able to stop as it was travelling so fast. I watched its tail lights disappearing down the road, but then something weird happened. It stopped about 300 yards away. I didn't move. He can't have stopped for me, I thought. I watched the stationary car; from where I was stood it looked like the driver was searching for something on the back seat. He's probably looking for a map or a snack, I thought. But then his lights came on again and I realised that he was reversing towards me. I picked up my rucksack and started walking. When he reached me I saw he had wound down the passenger window, so I stuck my head through it. The inside of the car was quite a sight. The driver was a small, swarthy, chubby little man. And he was naked except for a pair of Speedos and his flip-flops.

I asked where he was headed.

'Lyon,' came the reply, with a greasy grin. I asked him to open the boot for my bag and while I was at the back of the car I memorised the number plate. This was something I always did if a lift looked dodgy. Then I closed the boot and climbed into the passenger seat. As I got in, I noticed a neatly folded suit and shirt on the back seat. So that was what he'd been doing while he had been parked up: removing his suit. I stared straight ahead. This was really weird, but I needed the lift. I still had to get to Paris and then to the coast in just over a day. I gave him short, blunt answers, trying to get across the idea that I didn't want to talk. But he kept going. He had good English. Apparently, he had been down to see some friends in Nice for a party. He had intended to drive back to his house in Lyon the night before, but the party had been too much fun and now he was driving straight to his job in the city.

Eventually he took the hint and we drove in silence for 10 minutes. But then, out of the corner of my eye, I became aware of him wriggling around in his seat. He tapped my right arm. I looked round at him to find he had removed his Speedos and was pointing at his penis. It was tiny!

'You want to touch?' he asked, with that greasy grin again.

I looked down at his penis. It really was minuscule. I pointed at it and laughed, and the more I looked at it the more I laughed. This was obviously not the desired effect on his part. Or on his part, which seemed to shrink even further. We were doing

120 kilometres per hour down the dual carriageway. He then started to pull at his tiny todger. I had had enough.

'Right. Stop that right now,' I shouted. I then told him his number plate very calmly and very clearly.

'You are going to pull over at the next lay-by and you are going to get dressed. Then you are going to drive me to Lyon. Not to the centre of Lyon, not to the north of Lyon – to the start of the road to Paris. If you don't do this I will go to the nearest gendarmerie and tell them you tried to rape me. Do you understand?'

His grin was gone and he now looked very scared. He did exactly what I told him to do. For the rest of the trip, I stared out of the passenger window. When we reached the outskirts of Lyon, he started to protest that I was going to make him late for work, but I reminded him of my intentions regarding the police and he grudgingly drove me round the ring road in the rush-hour traffic. He finally dropped me at the junction for the A6 north. He was looking really stressed as he drove off. I often wonder what he told his boss when he finally reached his office.

From there I caught two lorries to the outskirts of Paris. This was my first ever visit to the French capital but I was finding it hard to get excited. Any capital city in the world is a lonely place without money, no matter how beautiful the buildings or how impressive the monuments. I found a Métro station at Gentilly but I had no money. I waited for someone to got through the gate and crashed through with them. I somehow got away with it. From there, I travelled to the Louvre and then walked to the British embassy, where I told them I hadn't eaten for two days. The gates opened and I was ushered inside. They gave me two Rich Tea biscuits and a cup of very weak tea to which I pointedly added seven teaspoons of sugar. They explained they couldn't help me financially. I begged and pleaded. The lack of sleep and the hunger must have made me very whiny because the guy eventually agreed to give me the 37p in francs that I would need to catch the Métro to Porte de la Chapelle, where the road to the Channel ports started. It took me three more lifts through the night to get to Calais.

I walked up and down the line of lorries telling my story to the drivers. Eventually one said I could get onto the boat in his cab; he would put me down as a second driver. I was on the ferry! I thanked him profusely and then headed to the cafe. If anyone left anything on their plate, I would try to get to it before the waitresses cleaned it up – I was that hungry. A middle-aged couple saw what I was doing – I wasn't exactly being subtle – and offered to buy me a full English breakfast. I had tears in my eyes as I thanked them. I have never tasted such an amazing breakfast in my life. As we neared Dover I went up on deck to watch the White Cliffs getting bigger. I was home.

From Dover I hitched along the south coast to Portsmouth, where I had started my journey nearly a month before, and then I headed up the A3 to Farnborough. It was so much easier to hitch in the UK than in France or Spain. I walked the last three miles from the motorway to my mum and dad's house on West Heath Road. My mum was in and was very surprised to see me. I had sent a postcard from Biarritz a couple of weeks before, and on it I had said I was going to spend the summer there. She made me a sandwich and I went upstairs and crashed out on the bed for 14 hours.

👍

Once I had recovered from my trip, about three days later, I hitched up to London. I went to Covent Garden and sat in awe as I watched the street acts there. Tim Batt was an amazing juggler who finished his act by juggling three lobster pots. Then there was Mac MacDonald, the Singing Jukebox. He had made a jukebox out of a cardboard box with a list of songs on it; when you dropped some money through the slot and pressed a song, Mac would push his head up through a hole in the box and sing that song. There was J. J. Waller who had a patter act; Duncan Trillo and Dave Brown, who were magicians; Terry St Clair and John Woodall, who played guitars; and Mike Mulkerrin, a very funny mime artist. There was Dave Spathaky, Howard Lee, Alex Dandrige and Chris Adams, who were all jugglers. John Lee was a slack-rope walker and Bernie a tightrope walker. There was an Iranian Charlie Chaplin impersonator who spoke little English and whom everyone called Charlie. There was also a Laurel and Hardy act by Andre Vincent and Richard Gauntlett; Andy Sinclair, a robotic act; Jon McKenna, the Pink Policeman; Patricia Martinelli from 'pap pap', a sketch show; Suki Webster and Fiona Freund, a female double act; John Lenahan, a magician; and Ollie and his breakdance crew. Sometimes Pookiesnackenburger would come up from Brighton with their comic musicals. These people were to become my new family.

There were two areas where you could perform in those days: inside or outside. The inside pitch was under the glass of the market at the Royal Opera House end and was run by the Covent Garden management team. You had to do a nerve-racking audition for them before you could gig there. They gave out spots at noon on a Monday in the form of a draw. Because of the space around the square performance area and the proximity of a cafe and some shops, you could attract a crowd of only about 150 people, some of them behind you, and so you performed in the round. The outside space was on the cobbles of the main piazza and was controlled by Alternative Arts. They booked their spots at 9am on a first come, first served basis. People would turn up earlier and earlier to be first in the queue, until one Sunday night there were five people already there at midnight. This was ridiculous. From then on, we made it a rule among ourselves that any act there at midnight would cut cards for who chose their spot first. A note was kept as each person turned up through the night. This was all right until the nights started getting colder, but we kept it up all through the winter. We would use the time to learn new skills or to sit and play poker. Sometimes new acts would grow out of conversations on those long winter nights. They would all teach me something over the next three years, whether it was a magic trick or a juggling move, how to ride a unicycle or a good bottling speech.

I should explain. In the olden days, street acts would send a friend round the crowd to collect money from the spectators. They would collect it in a leather bottle so that prying eyes couldn't see how much there was. After the act was finished, the money was counted and 10 per cent went to the bottler. When I first started at Covent Garden piazza, only the musical acts had bottlers; the rest of the performers would wait to the end of the show and then step forward and say their piece. This was a very important part of the show; you could be the most amazing juggler in the world, but if you did a poor bottling speech you'd go home with nothing. The best in the business was Mac MacDonald.

One day we were sitting under the portico of the Actors' Church, which was our proscenium arch at the cobblestoned end of the market. Opposite the portico was the Punch and Judy pub's balcony. This was a rich source of donations, as after a few drinks people become more generous. Mac had booked the 1pm slot outside and was looking miserably at the raindrops falling from the dark grey sky. He knew that if he went out in his jukebox the cardboard would get wet and be ruined, but this was his big slot of the week – the one he would use to pay for his food and bills. He prevaricated for about 10 minutes. Other people started to ask if they could have the slot as they didn't mind the rain. Mike Mulkerrin said, 'Why don't you just cut to the bottling speech?'

Mac looked thoughtful and then headed out into the rain. He gave the funniest, most moving bottling speech I had ever heard. It lasted nearly 30 minutes and involved him miming the reactions of his very young daughters when he returned home that evening without any bananas for them to eat. It was hilarious. A crowd began to form. He moved them under the cover of the market and called to the drinkers above to come out on the balcony. At the end, he wound up his speech: 'So if you could all now reach into your pockets, your wallets and your purses, take out your donation, fold it in half and place it in my hat, I would be most grateful.'

Genius. We all saw that comedy could be a good payer on the street. I stored that information away.

My act didn't go very well at first: I needed something different, something to make passers-by stop and watch. My outfit was a pair of size 14 hobnailed boots (the toes stuffed with newspaper), a pair of pink leggings and a white string vest. I had cut the collar and cuffs off a white dress shirt and I would wear them with a red bow tie, as if I had an invisible shirt. The whole ensemble was topped off by a grey fedora, which I would put brim up on the cobbles to collect any money.

I started by laying out lots of oranges in careful geometric shapes until I was standing in the middle of a circle. I would then pick up a single orange and with great panache I would throw it from one hand to the other, then bow and stay down, waiting for the applause. I never got any. I would then get whoever had gathered to watch to cheer and clap, which would draw attention to the show going on and attract more people. I would pick up a second orange, throw them both in the air and catch them again. Then I would do it one-handed. I would then bow again, and again I would wait for the applause. The third orange would get a laugh as I would juggle two side by side with my right hand and move the third up and down clasped firmly in my left hand. Then I would bow again. When the crowd started to clap this time I would break into a three-ball routine, doing cascades and bouncing oranges off my elbow and my knee, rolling one over my head, catching one on the back of my neck and flicking it back into the juggling pattern. Then I would juggle four oranges.

Next I would pick up a box of six eggs and announce that my next trick would be to keep all six eggs in the air at the same time. This would elicit some oohs from the crowd. I would close the box firmly, throw the box up in the air and catch it a few times. I'd get a lot of groans for that. I would then explain that I could make the six eggs disappear. I would produce a pint glass and, with a lot of ceremony, I'd break all six into the glass. As the audience counted down from five, I would drink all six in a couple of seconds (I have never been as healthy as I was then). Then I would produce three pig's kidneys, which would send a few people scurrying away but could also attract a bigger crowd – I never knew which from one show to the next. Some people complained that they were showered with blood, but most knew to get out of the way! This was Punk Juggling. I would finish this section by catching a kidney in my mouth. If it was a hot day the kidneys could get a bit claggy if I did more than one show, but on other days I would take them home and have them for my tea (if I hadn't dropped them, of course). I would finish by juggling a peanut, an orange and a watermelon – this is obviously very difficult because of the different weights. I would announce that I would finish by catching the peanut in my mouth, but after a few cascades I would throw the watermelon high into the air and as it began to fall I would swear and it would break on the top of my head. I would then do a two-minute bottling speech, hat in hand.

I think my record bottle was £32, which was quite a lot in those days. The following summer I joined up with John Woodall, a posh lad from Gerrards Cross who always looked like a rock star. He would wear white jeans to perform, and as we were hanging out and working on the street I'll never know how he kept them so clean. He played a guitar plugged into a little Vox speaker. During the Monday-morning queue we came up with an idea for an act: we decided that John would play songs and I would do mime dancing to them. For 'Space Oddity', I had a cardboard box with a square cut out on one side; when John sang 'Put your helmet on' I would place it on my head. For the line 'Here am I, floating round my tin can' I would run to the nearest bin and grab an empty can and walk round it in slow motion. For 'Planet earth is blue' I would pull an exaggerated sad face. You get the picture.

For 'Vincent (Starry, Starry Night)', I would get a woman from the crowd and stand her slightly in front of the rest of the audience. Then I would fetch a large drawing pad and a black marker pen and would make a big deal of drawing the woman, holding the pen horizontal at arm's length as if calculating the perspective. When John finished, I would turn the pad round to reveal a picture of a stick person in a triangular skirt.

For 'Sorrow', I would steal a handbag or a backpack from someone and run off to the north side of the market. I would run down the side and then cut through the market and back along the south side so I could appear on the other side of the piazza just as the song finished, when I would give the bag back.

It may seem strange, but we were the highest-earning act in Covent Garden in December 1983. This was good news – I had been living hand to mouth up until then. When I first moved to London I had been travelling up from Farnborough, but then Pete Carey offered me a sofa to sleep on. He was living with Jonathan Bell, Mike Pantling and Rick Garrett, all from the grammar school. They had a council flat in quite a rough estate in Hackney (someone was hit with an axe on our landing, and survived). In the flat by the front door they had a phone room that was five feet by seven and had nothing in it but a sofa and a phone. The sofa folded down into a bed, but the bed touched both walls and you couldn't open the door. This was where I lived for a year, without paying them any rent. I tried to

stay out at Covent Garden as much as possible. It must have been a pain in the arse for the four of them and I'd like to apologise to them profusely, but they gave me the time I needed to get my act together. I hope I can make it up to them with some of the money I receive for this book!

John and I worked together for six happy months as Soft Shoe Shuffle, but in the spring he told me of his plans to go to the south of France with his French girlfriend. I was heartbroken at the news and guessed I would have to go back to the juggling, which would never be as lucrative as the double act.

One afternoon as I sat under the portico I began talking to Angelo Abela. He was doing a comedy act with a guitarist called John, too, and I had occasionally bottled for them during their act to make some extra money. His John was Australian and had decided to return home as his visa had expired, so I suggested Angelo and I get together as a double act. We worked out a few routines and did them one morning in the inside spot, improvising between skits. We mimed different circus acts very badly and called ourselves Circus Berkus. Gradually we moved on to miming famous films in three-minute sketches and changed our name to The Vicious Boys. Angelo was shorter than me, athletic, with black hair. I was tall, skinny and dyed my hair blonde to accentuate the difference between us. We loved making up new film parodies.

That July, after I had taken Angelo to his first Pamplona, we returned to Covent Garden and won the *Time Out* Street Entertainer of the Year award.

But that is another story.

Acknowledgements

I could not have written this book without the support and love of the following people.

Firstly, Andrea: thank you for being my love and my best friend.

I'd like to thank Grace Smart and Joe Shavin, who constantly make me a proud dad.

I also need to say a big thank you to my brother Neil and my sister Rosalind. They have always been there for me.

I would like to thank all those I went to school with at Cove Manor Infants, Cove Manor Junior, Farnborough Grammar School and Farnborough Sixth Form College, both the teachers and the students. If you didn't get a mention in the book, I'm sorry (unless you were one of the bullies!)

A big thank you to Skip Graham Gorvin and John Sherwin, two leaders who took boys and turned them into fine young men.

I would like to thank those who 'studied' with me at Notre Dame and Christs College in Liverpool. Especially Ged Smith, Tony Wretham, Matt and Mary Battersby, Denise Souffi, Keith Seed, Moira and Tony Flannery, Catherine Robinson, Rose Core and Brendan Routledge.

Thanks too to Bob Hornby, who encouraged me so much and shared his comprehensive knowledge of theatre with me.

A big shout out to Samuel Beckett, Lord (David) Steel and Guy Garvey.

Thank you, Ian McArdle, for teaching me to juggle. My whole career has been down to you! Oh, and all at 489 TIE.

Also, a big thank you to Pella, Stefan, Cabot, Marsha and Wrigleys for looking after me in Biarritz.

Obviously I wouldn't be where I am today without the help and inspiration of all the characters at Covent Garden piazza in the early 1980s, both the acts and those at Alternative Arts. I am indebted to all of you.

To Mike Pantling, Jonathan Bell, Rick Garrett and Peter Carey, who literally gave me a home for a year; I cannot thank you enough.

To Ted Pearce (23 seasons as manager. There will never be another!) and all at Farnborough Town FC and Farnborough FC – thanks for the ups and downs over the years.

To John Woodall for being so cool.

To Angelo Abela: thank you for all the laughs and adventures. You helped me move indoors from the street.

A big thank you to The Comedy Store Players, with whom I perform every Wednesday and Sunday, and to Don Ward, who owns The Comedy Store.

Thanks to Paul and Andy and all involved with the Hawksbee and Jacobs Show on TalkSport for letting me tell my stories.

Cheers to Phil Carroll and Donna Wood, and all at AA Publishing for giving me the chance to write this book.

Lastly I'd like to thank anyone who may have given me a lift between 1977 and 1982. You didn't have to. But your kindness allowed me to be who I wanted to be.